Autism: Understanding the Spectrum, Embracing the Journey

Adinda Nezma Meidina
Nafilah Ramadhanti
Raisa Qonita
M. Aditya Nugraha
Nabila Az-zahra Hasibuan
Dyah Fatha Istiqomah
Putri Salsabillah
Muhammad Valdis Muyassar
Akbar Triandra
Yolanda Delia Putri

Department of Medicine, Faculty of Medicine,
Sriwijaya University

ACKNOWLEDGEMENTS

I would like to express my gratitude to God Almighty for His blessings and grace, which have enabled the successful completion of this book. This book is designed to provide a deeper understanding of autism through comprehensive explanations in each chapter and sub-chapter. It begins with an introduction to what Autism Spectrum Disorder (ASD) is, its causes and risk factors, and continues with the diagnosis, interventions, and support needed by individuals with autism. Each section of this book is carefully crafted to provide clear, evidence-based insights so that readers can better understand the autism spectrum in a broader context.

I would also like to thank all those who have contributed to the preparation of this book, including researchers, professionals, and practitioners, for their invaluable support and knowledge. Your dedication and hard work in advancing our understanding of autism have made this book possible. Without your contributions, this book would not have come to fruition.

I hope this book will benefit readers by enhancing their understanding of autism, both scientifically and practically. I trust that the information presented will help raise awareness, reduce stigma, and provide guidance for those working with individuals with autism. It is my hope that this book will serve as a valuable source of knowledge in supporting our shared role in creating a more inclusive society and fostering a better understanding of autism.

CONTENTS

LIST OF FIGURES

LIST OF TABLES

CHAPTER 1: UNDERSTANDING AUTISM

Nafilah Ramadhanti, Department of Medicine, Faculty of Medicine, Sriwijaya University

A. Defining Autism Spectrum Disorder (ASD)

Autism is a developmental condition that emerges during early childhood, marked by challenges in communication, social interaction, rigid behaviors, and repetitive activities. Autism Spectrum Disorder (ASD) is currently classified into three main categories: Autism Disorder (classic autism), Asperger's Syndrome, and PDD-NOS (Pervasive Developmental Disorder-Not Otherwise Specified) (American Psychiatric Association, 2022). ASD is a neurobiological condition shaped by both genetic and environmental factors that impact brain development (Hodges, 2020).

B. Why Is It Called a "Spectrum"?

The concept of autism as a spectrum emphasizes the distinct ways it manifests in each individual. Although diagnostic manuals like the DSM offer broad criteria, the complexity of autism goes beyond a simple list of symptoms. This suggests that no two individuals with autism have the same experiences or behaviors, showcasing the diversity within the spectrum (Rosen, 2021).

The Evolution of Autism Diagnosis

Autism was first described in 1943 by Leo Kanner as an emotional disturbance unrelated to cognition, and soon after, it was classified as a form of childhood schizophrenia in the DSM (Lordan, 2021). The 1987 revision of DSM-III introduced pervasive developmental disorder-not otherwise specified (PDD-NOS) as part of autism diagnoses, setting the stage for a broader understanding of autism, though the term "spectrum" was not yet used (Mintz, 2016).

Autism Recognized as a Spectrum

The DSM-IV, released in 1994, was the first edition to recognize autism as a spectrum, including five conditions: autism, PDD-NOS, Asperger's syndrome, childhood disintegrative disorder

(CDD), and Rett's syndrome (Rosen, 2021). The DSM-5, the most recent edition, introduced Autism Spectrum Disorder (ASD), defined by "persistent difficulties in reciprocal social communication and interaction" along with "restricted, repetitive behaviour patterns" (American Psychiatric Association, 2022). This update reinforced the view of autism as a continuous spectrum in contemporary medical practice.

C. Epidemiology of Autism Spectrum Disorder (ASD)

Recent epidemiological studies in the United States indicate that ASD affects 1 in 36 children by the age of 8, with males being about four times more likely to be diagnosed than females (Maenner, 2023). However, girls meeting the criteria for ASD are at higher risk of being undiagnosed or misdiagnosed. The female autism phenotype, characterized by subtler symptoms and social "camouflaging," may contribute to delayed or overlooked diagnoses (Hodges, 2020).

ASD is found across all racial, ethnic, and socioeconomic groups, but its diagnosis is not evenly distributed (Baio, 2018). In earlier years, ASD prevalence was 50% higher among White children compared to Black or Hispanic children. Over time, these disparities diminished, with prevalence among Black children equaling that of White children in 2016 and Hispanic children reaching parity in 2018 (Maenner, 2021). Factors such as stigma, limited access to healthcare, and non-English primary languages may contribute to the ongoing disparity (Hodges, 2020).

D. Myths and Misconceptions About Autism

Misconceptions about autism can have a negative impact on families by preventing them from accessing the proper education and treatment. These misunderstandings can delay diagnosis, foster feelings of guilt, and result in the adoption of ineffective or harmful interventions, all of which hinder the family's ability to provide the necessary support for their child's development. Therefore, all sectors of society must collaborate to enhance understanding of autism and dismantle its misconceptions.

Lack of Interest in Social Relationships

The truth is, individuals with autism generally want to form relationships (Cresswell, 2019), but their difficulties with social communication can create challenges in interacting with neurotypical people (Grace, 2022). This often leads to negative social experiences, including loneliness, bullying, exclusion, and stigma (Boucher, 2023). Autistic children perceive loneliness in a way that differs from non-autistic children (Grace, 2022). Studies have found that autistic children associate loneliness mainly with being alone, whereas non-autistic children view it as a combination of emotional and social-cognitive loneliness (Hymas, 2022).

Low Cognitive Intelligence

Epidemiological studies from various countries show a significant prevalence of intellectual disability (ID) among children with Autism Spectrum Disorder (ASD). In the United States, recent data indicates that 35% of 8-year-old children with ASD have an IQ below 70 (American Psychiatric Association, 2022). Otherwise, there's also autistic individuals that often display exceptional abilities, such as special isolated skills (SIS) and perceptual peaks (PP), though their prevalence varies (Meilleur, 2015). Nearly half (46%) of the children had at least one parent-reported talent, with an additional 23% having personal strengths (Bal, 2022).

Vaccination

The association between vaccines and autism is often influenced by the timing of autism diagnoses, which typically occur after children receive their main childhood immunizations. However, a study found no increased risk of autism associated with the MMR vaccination. It also concluded that the vaccine does not trigger autism in susceptible individuals, and there is no clustering of ASD cases following MMR vaccination (Hviid, 2019). A meta-analysis, along with numerous individual studies, further confirmed that there is no correlation between MMR vaccination and ASD (Taylor, 2014).

Concerns about the use of thimerosal-containing vaccines and its potential link to ASD have been raised due to the established connection between ASD and organic mercury (Gabis, 2022). In fact, numerous peer-reviewed studies and meta-analyses have found no increased risk of ASD associated with thimerosal exposure in vaccines (DeStefano, 2019). Despite scientific evidence disproving this connection, the anti-mercury movement continued, even after thimerosal was removed from vaccines, as autism rates still rose (Davidson, 2017).

References

American Psychiatric Association. (2022). *Diagnostic and Statistical Manual of Mental Disorders* (5th-TR). American Psychiatric Association.

Baio, J., Wiggins, L., Christensen, D. L., Maenner, M. J. (2018). Prevalence of Autism Spectrum Disorder Among Children Aged 8 Years — Autism and Developmental Disabilities Monitoring Network, 11 Sites, United States, 2014. *MMWR. Surveillance Summaries, 67*(6), 1–23. https://doi.org/10.15585/mmwr.ss6706a1

Bal, V. H., Wilkinson, E., & Fok, M. (2022). Cognitive profiles of children with autism spectrum disorder with parent-reported extraordinary talents and personal strengths. *Autism : the international journal of research and practice, 26*(1), 62–74. https://doi.org/10.1177/13623613211020618

Boucher, T. Q., Lukacs, J. N., Scheerer, N. E., & Iarocci, G. (2023). Negative first impression judgements of autistic children by non-autistic adults. *Frontiers in psychiatry, 14,* 1241584. https://doi.org/10.3389/fpsyt.2023.1241584

Davidson M. (2017). Vaccination as a cause of autism-myths and controversies. *Dialogues in clinical neuroscience, 19*(4), 403–407. https://doi.org/10.31887/DCNS.2017.19.4/mdavidson

DeStefano, F., Bodenstab, H. M., & Offit, P. A. (2019). Principal

Controversies in Vaccine Safety in the United States. *Clinical infectious diseases : an official publication of the Infectious Diseases Society of America, 69*(4), 726–731. https://doi.org/10.1093/cid/ciz135

Gabis, L. V., Attia, O. L., Goldman, M., Barak, N., Tefera, P., Shefer, S., Shaham, M., & Lerman-Sagie, T. (2022). The myth of vaccination and autism spectrum. *European journal of paediatric neurology : EJPN : official journal of the European Paediatric Neurology Society, 36*, 151–158. https://doi.org/10.1016/j.ejpn.2021.12.011

Gibbs, V., & Pellicano, E. (2023). "Maybe we just seem like easy targets": A qualitative analysis of autistic adults' experiences of interpersonal violence. *Autism, 27*(7), 136236132211503. https://doi.org/10.1177/13623613221150375

Grace, K., Remington, A., Lloyd-Evans, B., Davies, J., & Crane, L. (2022). Loneliness in autistic adults: A systematic review. *Autism : the international journal of research and practice, 26*(8), 2117–2135. https://doi.org/10.1177/13623613221077721

Hodges, H., Fealko, C., & Soares, N. (2020). Autism spectrum disorder: definition, epidemiology, causes, and clinical evaluation. *Translational pediatrics, 9*(Suppl 1), S55–S65. https://doi.org/10.21037/tp.2019.09.09

Hviid, A., Hansen, J. V., Frisch, M., & Melbye, M. (2019). Measles, mumps, rubella vaccination and autism. *Annals of Internal Medicine, 170*(8), 513–520. https://doi.org/10.7326/m18-2101

Hymas, R., Badcock, J. C., & Milne, E. (2022). Loneliness in autism and its association with anxiety and depression: A systematic review with meta-analyses. *Review Journal of Autism and Developmental Disorders*, 1-36.

Lordan, R. (2021). *Autism Spectrum Disorders* (A. M. Grabrucker, Ed.). Exon Publications. https://doi.org/10.36255/exonpublications.autismspectrumdisor

ders.2021

Maenner, M. J., Shaw, K. A., Bakian, A. V. (2021). Prevalence and Characteristics of Autism Spectrum Disorder Among Children Aged 8 Years — Autism and Developmental Disabilities Monitoring Network, 11 Sites, United States, 2018. MMWR. Surveillance Summaries, 70(11), 1–16.

Maenner, M. J., Warren, Z., Williams, A. R. (2023). Prevalence and Characteristics of Autism Spectrum Disorder Among Children Aged 8 Years - Autism and Developmental Disabilities Monitoring Network, 11 Sites, United States, 2020. Morbidity and mortality weekly report. Surveillance summaries (Washington, D.C. : 2002), 72(2), 1–14. https://doi.org/10.15585/mmwr.ss7202a1

Meilleur, A. A., Jelenic, P., & Mottron, L. (2015). Prevalence of clinically and empirically defined talents and strengths in autism. *Journal of autism and developmental disorders, 45*(5), 1354–1367. https://doi.org/10.1007/s10803-014-2296-2

Mintz, M. (2016). Evolution in the Understanding of Autism Spectrum Disorder: Historical Perspective. The Indian Journal of Pediatrics, 84(1), 44–52. https://doi.org/10.1007/s12098-016-2080-8

Rosen, N. E., Lord, C., & Volkmar, F. R. (2021). The Diagnosis of Autism: From Kanner to DSM-III to DSM-5 and Beyond. *Journal of autism and developmental disorders, 51*(12), 4253–4270. https://doi.org/10.1007/s10803-021-04904-1

Taylor, L. E., Swerdfeger, A. L., & Eslick, G. D. (2014). Vaccines are not associated with autism: an evidence-based meta-analysis of case-control and cohort studies. *Vaccine, 32*(29), 3623–3629. https://doi.org/10.1016/j.vaccine.2014.04.085

CHAPTER 2: CAUSES AND RISK FACTORS

Raisa Qonita, Department of Medicine, Faculty of Medicine, Sriwijaya University

A. Understanding the Genetics of Autism

Recent advances in the genetics of neurodevelopmental disorders (NDD) have led to the identification of over 1,500 genes linked to conditions like intellectual disability and autism. Current research focuses on understanding the functions of these genes to reveal the biological processes that affect the clinical outcomes for individuals carrying mutations (Leblond et al., 2021).

A study conducted by Satterstrom et al. (2020) employed whole-exome sequencing (WES) on parent-offspring trios from a cohort of 60 patients, predominantly diagnosed with syndromic intellectual disability (ID) or autism spectrum disorder (ASD). This study identified eight pathogenic variants in genes previously linked to ID/ASD, including SYNGAP1, SMAD6, PACS1, SHANK3, KMT2A, KCNQ2, ACTB, and POGZ. Additionally, it discovered four de novo disruptive variants in four novel candidate genes associated with ASD/ID: MBP, PCDHA1, PCDH15, and PDPR.

B. Environmental Influences and Their Impact

The rapid industrial growth seen in recent decades has resulted in the release of substantial amounts of pollutants into the environment, creating challenges for both healthcare professionals and ecologists. These metals toxicity disrupts cellular metabolism by inducing oxidative stress, leading to damage to DNA, lipids, and proteins. Excessive exposure to heavy metals is a well-established risk factor for conditions like type II diabetes, certain cancers, hormonal imbalances, and neurological disorders. Recently, there has been growing attention within the scientific community regarding the role of lead, particularly its potential link to the development of autism spectrum disorders A meta-analysis by Stojsavljević et al. (2023) compares lead levels in biological samples (such as hair, blood, and urine) from children with autism and neurotypical children as controls. The analysis found significantly higher lead concentrations in all biological samples from children with ASD, suggesting a connection between environmental lead exposure and the subsequent diagnosis of autism in children (Yenkoyan et al., 2024). Similarly, another study identified a significant relationship between mercury concentration and autism (Jafari Mohammadabadi et al., 2020).

Further research has explored the potential role of air pollution in neurodevelopmental and neurodegenerative disorders, including ASD and Alzheimer's disease. Human studies suggest that maternal exposure to particulate matter (PM2.5) during pregnancy may heighten the risk of ASD in offspring (Win-Shwe et al., 2021).

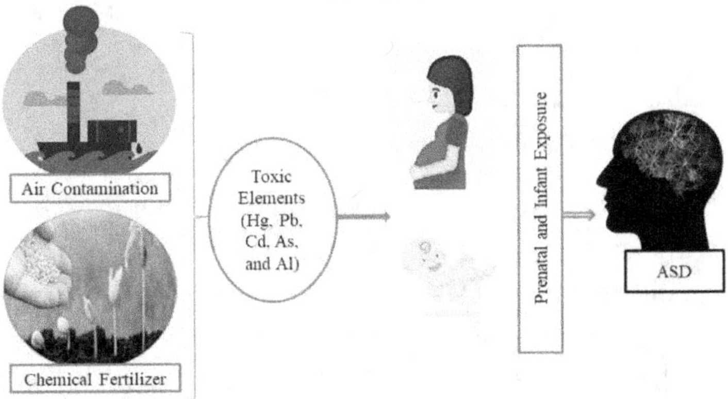

Figure 2.1. Association between exposures to toxic elements and ASD (Shiani et al., 2023)

Present study examined toxic metal levels in various biological samples from individuals with and without ASD. The significant rise in ASD prevalence suggests that exposure to toxic chemicals, including heavy metals, may play a role in its development. The most commonly identified toxicants were mercury (Hg), lead (Pb), cadmium (Cd), arsenic (As), and aluminum (Al). While the exact causes of autism remain uncertain and widely debated, environmental factors have been acknowledged as contributing influences (Shiani et al., 2023).

C. The Debate Around Prenatal and Perinatal Factors

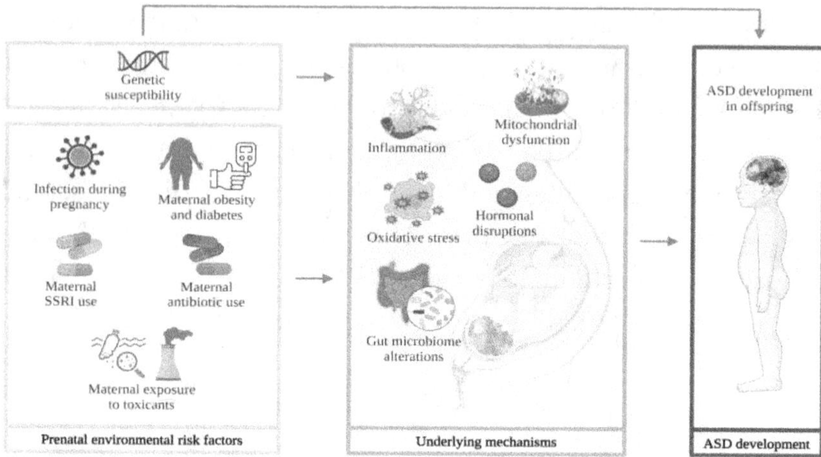

Figure 2.2. Prenatal environmental risk factors for ASD (Love et al., 2024)

Over the past few decades, numerous studies have sought to identify the causes of ASD, yet the exact mechanisms behind its development remain unclear. A study from Birth asphyxia has been linked to a more than thirteen-fold increased risk of ASD. Breastfeeding difficulties have also been associated with a higher risk of the disorder. Parenting styles, particularly low responsiveness (LR) and harsh or neglectful parenting, have been connected to an elevated risk of ASD in children. Additionally, harsh parenting and maternal fever during pregnancy have been identified as risk factors (Yuan et al., 2024).

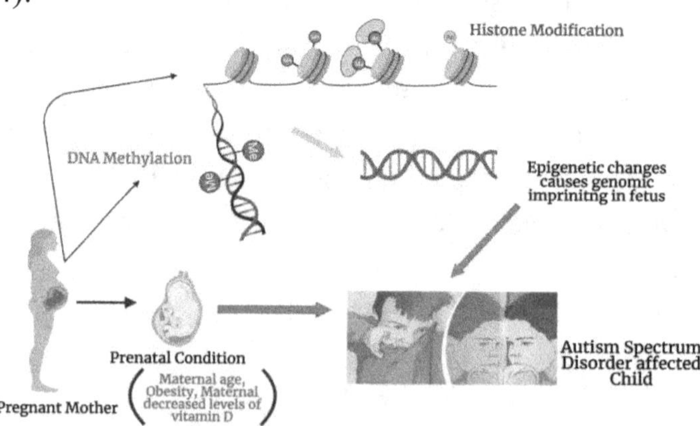

Figure 2.3. Epigenetic changes influenced by maternal factors (Balachandar et al.,

2022)

Research suggests that two key predictors of a child being diagnosed with autism are maternal and infant-related factors during the perinatal period. Maternal factors include any illness during pregnancy, gestational diabetes, or type 2 diabetes. Infant-related factors include issues like the umbilical cord around the neck during labor, infant distress during labor, injury during labor, and low birth weight (Mahboub et al., 2023).

Another study highlights that histone modification may occur during fetal neurodevelopment in the womb, either through acylation or methylation at the histone tail. Additionally, DNA methylation could result from changes in the location of DNMT3a and DNMT3b enzymes in the embryo. These potential modifications may lead to genomic imprinting in the fetus, which could contribute to the onset of autism spectrum disorder (ASD) in offspring (Balachandar et al., 2022).

D. Dispelling False Claims About Vaccines and Autism

In the 1990s, a study was published in the Lancet journal that suggested a possible connection between the MMR vaccine and autism. The study, which involved only 12 children, did not establish a causal link between the vaccine and autism. Additionally, the research was found to contain numerous flaws, inaccuracies, and fabrications. Once these issues were revealed, the journal officially retracted the paper (UNICEF, 2024).

Despite the abundant evidence disproving any link between vaccines and autism, and the absence of reliable studies supporting such a connection, skepticism to vaccines persists due to distrust in the scientific data being presented. The spread of such theories heightens fear, which can have harmful consequences for public health (Gabis et al., 2022). One study found that there were 16.5% of parents who believed that vaccinations is a possible cause of ASD. This was the fourth most commonly cited potential cause by respondents, following genetic factors, environmental exposures, and complications during birth or delivery (Fombonne et al., 2020).

Since symptoms of autism often emerge around the time children receive the MMR vaccine, some parents may fear that the vaccine causes autism. However, experts in vaccine safety from the CDC confirms that the MMR vaccine is not linked to the rise in autism diagnoses (CDC, 2024)

Reference

Balachandar, V., Mahalaxmi, I., Neethu, R., Arul, N., & Abhilash, V. G. (2022). New insights into epigenetics as an influencer: An associative study between maternal prenatal factors in Autism Spectrum Disorder (ASD). *Neurology Perspectives*, *2*(2), 78–86. https://doi.org/10.1016/j.neurop.2022.01.002

CDC. (2024). *Measles, Mumps, Rubella (MMR) Vaccine Safety*. Vaccine Safety. https://www.cdc.gov/vaccine-safety/vaccines/mmr.html

Fombonne, E., Goin-Kochel, R. P., O'Roak, B. J., & Consortium, the S. (2020). Beliefs in vaccine as causes of autism among SPARK cohort caregivers. *Vaccine*, *38*(7), 1794. https://doi.org/10.1016/j.vaccine.2019.12.026

Gabis, L. V., Attia, O. L., Goldman, M., Barak, N., Tefera, P., Shefer, S., Shaham, M., & Lerman-Sagie, T. (2022). The myth of vaccination and autism spectrum. *European Journal of Paediatric Neurology*, *36*, 151–158. https://doi.org/10.1016/j.ejpn.2021.12.011

Jafari Mohammadabadi, H., Rahmatian, A., Sayehmiri, F., & Rafiei, M. (2020). The Relationship Between the Level of Copper, Lead, Mercury and Autism Disorders: A Meta-Analysis. *Pediatric Health, Medicine and Therapeutics*, *Volume 11*, 369–378. https://doi.org/10.2147/phmt.s210042

Leblond, C. S., Le, T.-L., Malesys, S., Cliquet, F., Tabet, A.-C., Delorme, R., Rolland, T., & Bourgeron, T. (2021). Operative list of genes associated with autism and neurodevelopmental disorders based on database review. *Molecular and Cellular Neuroscience,* *113,* 103623. https://doi.org/10.1016/j.mcn.2021.103623

Love, C., Sominsky, L., O'Hely, M., Berk, M., Vuillermin, P., & Dawson, S. L. (2024). Prenatal environmental risk factors for autism spectrum disorder and their potential mechanisms. *BMC Medicine, 22*(1), 393. https://doi.org/10.1186/s12916-024-03617-3

Mahboub, S., Al-Suhaibani, S., Ellatif, H. A., & Elkholi, S. M. (2023). Maternal- and child-related risk factors for autism during the perinatal period. *Middle East Current Psychiatry, 30*(1), 53. https://doi.org/10.1186/s43045-023-00326-0

Satterstrom, F. K., Kosmicki, J. A., Wang, J., Breen, M. S., Rubeis, S. D., An, J.-Y., Peng, M., Collins, R., Grove, J., Klei, L., Stevens, C., Reichert, J., Mulhern, M. S., Artomov, M., Gerges, S., Sheppard, B., Xu, X., Bhaduri, A., Norman, U., … Buxbaum, J. D. (2020). Large-Scale Exome Sequencing Study Implicates Both Developmental and Functional Changes in the Neurobiology of Autism. *Cell, 180*(3), 568-584.e23. https://doi.org/10.1016/j.cell.2019.12.036

Shiani, A., Sharafi, K., Omer, A. K., Kiani, A., Karamimatin, B., Massahi, T., & Ebrahimzadeh, G. (2023). A systematic literature review on the association between exposures to toxic elements and an autism spectrum disorder. *Science of The Total Environment, 857,* 159246. https://doi.org/10.1016/j.scitotenv.2022.159246Aleksandar

Stojsavljević, Novak Lakićević, & Slađan Pavlović. (2023). Does Lead Have a Connection to Autism? A Systematic Review and Meta-Analysis. *Toxics, 11*(9), 753–753. https://doi.org/10.3390/toxics11090753

UNICEF Europe and Central Asia. (2024). Retrieved December 12, 2024, from https://www.unicef.org/eca/stories/yes-mmr-vaccine-safe

Win-Shwe, T.-T., Kyi-Tha-Thu, C., Fujitani, Y., Tsukahara, S., & Hirano, S. (2021). Perinatal Exposure to Diesel Exhaust-Origin Secondary Organic Aerosol Induces Autism-Like Behavior in Rats. *International Journal of Molecular Sciences*, *22*(2), 538. https://doi.org/10.3390/ijms22020538

Yenkoyan, K., Mkhitaryan, M., & Bjørklund, G. (n.d.). Environmental Risk Factors in Autism Spectrum Disorder: A Narrative Review. *Http://Www.Eurekaselect.Com*. Retrieved December 12, 2024, from https://www.eurekaselect.com/article/137178

Yuan, J., Zhao, Y., Lan, X., Zhang, Y., & Zhang, R. (2024). Prenatal, perinatal and parental risk factors for autism spectrum disorder in China: A case- control study. *BMC Psychiatry*, *24*, 219. https://doi.org/10.1186/s12888-024-05643-0

CHAPTER 3 : SIGN AND SYMPTOMS OF AUTISM

M. Aditya Nugraha, Department of Medicine, Faculty of Medicine, Sriwijaya University

A. Early indicators of Autism in Childhood

Although the diagnosis of ASD can be done at the age of 3 years, early signs of autism can be observed even under the age of 1 year. The urgency in understanding and knowing these early signs is to carry out early management and prevent late diagnosis. Early indicators of autism can be seen based on the following areas:

Attention differences

Disturbances in attention development are a characteristic of autism that affect a child's ability to focus on the surrounding environment. Children diagnosed with autism often show signs of a lack of response to social stimuli (responsiveness to nicknames and applause) and non-social stimuli (rattles) (Turki Abualait et al., 2024).

In a test, children with ASD were found to be more interested in geometric shapes visually than social images, failed to respond to speech sounds, and failed in non-social aspects. This suggests that children with ASD may show disturbances in basic orientation, especially towards social stimuli (Mash et al., 2014).

Disturbances and failures in responding to social stimuli hypothetically contribute to joint attention disorders. By definition, joint attention is the ability to engage in a social context by sharing experiences and interests about objects and events with others. This ability is very important in the development of spoken language. Normally, at the age of 6 and 9 months, children will learn to share attention by looking between objects and caregivers. Furthermore, at the age of 9 months to 12 months, children will learn to share attention with movements such as pointing. In children with ASD, there is a disruption in the initiation of joint attention in the form of failure to coordinate gaze, movement, and facial expressions (Mash et al., 2014).

Prelinguistic communication development

Prelinguistic development refers to the period of a child's development before they have a linguistic system to acquire language. Prelinguistic communication is how children communicate before they learn language. Prelinguistic communication can be in the form of gestures, facial expressions, and body language (Rantalainen et al., 2021).

Children with ASD often have difficulty understanding and expressing themselves nonverbally, such as limited facial expressions and eye contact. This can hinder their ability to develop basic communication skills such as the use of gestures and emotional expression (Soetjiningsih, 2013).

Research shows that delays in prelinguistic movements such as using gestures, facial expressions, and eye contact can negatively impact future speech and verbal communication skills. This can lead to broader impairments in language and communication development in children with ASD (Soetjiningsih, 2013).

Affective expression and Temperament

In children with ASD, some show sudden changes in mood and emotions such as crying or laughing for no reason. Children may also be temperamental and easily angered. Excessive fear of objects that are not scary, severe separation anxiety and also severe depression can be found in autistic children (Departemen Psikiatri FKUI, 2017).

Sensory response and interest

Children with ASD often experience variations in sensory responses. These differences can be in the form of hypersensitivity to repeated stimuli or hypersensitivity to new stimuli. In addition, some also experience a lack of sensitivity to coordination between sensors which results in impaired sensory integration (Turki Abualait et al., 2024).

Sensory hypersensitivity can be in the form of hyperacusis (hypersensitivity to sound) so that children will cover their ears if they hear loud sounds. Visual manifestations can also occur in the form of bright lights that make children tense and uncomfortable or even make children like the light. While hyposensitivity causes children to become insensitive such as when children are injured, children do not cry (Departemen Psikiatri FKUI, 2017).

3.1.5 Motor skills Development and object exploration

Motor problems are a sign and symptom of ASD. These motor disorders can be in the form of motor stereotypies, repetitive activities and interests, and disorders of motor control and coordination (Posar & Visconti, 2022).

The majority of children with ASD show stereotypes and limitations such as clapping their hands and shaking their bodies. Some children also experience motor coordination disorders such as tip toe walking, clumsiness, difficulty learning to tie shoelaces, difficulty brushing their teeth, difficulty cutting food, and difficulty buttoning clothes. (Departemen Psikiatri FKUI, 2017).

Disturbances in object exploration are also experienced by children with ASD. Children with ASD show reduced exploration behavior seen at the age of 10 months (Turki Abualait et al., 2024).

B. Recognizing Symptoms Across Different Age Groups

Infancy

Symptoms of ASD can actually be observed starting from infancy under one year of age. Typical symptoms can include a lack of response to sound and limited eye contact. Babies with ASD also tend to show a low desire for interaction, for example rarely smiling or not responding to other people's expressions and also ASD babies experience gross and fine motor delays which are usually often complained about by parents of babies (J. Wolff & Piven, 2020).

Childhood

About 50% of children with ASD experience normal development until the age of 1.5 to 3 years after which autistic symptoms can be observed by both family and doctors. In early childhood (toddlerhood), children with ASD usually experience:(Soetjiningsih, 2013).

a. Behavioral disorders

Behavioral disorders can include self-stimulation (odd repetitive movements or aimless behavior), self-injury, sleep disorders, eating disorders, hyper/hypoactivity, and attention disorders. In addition, ASD children also experience perseverative behavior or routine attitudes every day.

b. Social interaction disorder

Children with ASD do not respond when called so that parents assume that their child is deaf. Children also often avoid social interactions and tend to prefer playing alone rather than with other children.

c. Communication disorders

Children with ASD experience both verbal and non-verbal disorders, so they will have problems in communication. This is also caused by speech delays or difficulty in using language for communication.

d. Cognitive impairment

Cognitive impairment in ASD children does not affect all cognitive sectors. It is proven that some ASD children have extraordinary abilities in music and mathematics. In addition, due to slow language development, autistic children utter words that cannot be understood, imitate without understanding the meaning (ecolalism), and a monotone tone of voice like a robot. Children also experience disorders in communication, both verbal and non-verbal.

   e. Abnormal sensing response

Children with ASD often exhibit high sensory sensitivity, such as being bothered by loud noises or certain textures.

   f. Emotional disturbance

Emotional disturbance here is in the form of feelings that suddenly change in children with ASD. And sometimes there is excessive fear of things that are not scary. Children also show a lack of response to other people's emotions and are unable to show empathy

In school-age children, ASD symptoms include difficulty understanding social rules, such as sharing or taking turns in games. Children with ASD may have unusual communication patterns, such as speaking in a monotone or talking at length about favorite topics without paying attention to others' responses. They often have difficulty forming and maintaining friendships and exhibit high sensory sensitivities, such as being bothered by loud noises or certain textures. Academic difficulties, especially those related to organizational skills and attention, also often emerge at this stage (Almsmary et al., 2022).

Puberty

When they reach adolescence, the challenges they face become more complex. Teenagers with ASD often feel isolated because of difficulty building interpersonal relationships. They can also experience emotional problems, such as social anxiety or depression. Their repetitive behaviors and special interests usually become more intense and more visible than their peers. Complex social situations are often difficult for them to understand, especially amidst increasing social pressure during puberty (Soetjiningsih, 2013).

At this time, autistic children sometimes experience seizures for the first time during puberty due to the hormonal mechanisms that occur. In addition, many of the behavioral problems that have been mentioned become more severe and more frequent. Autistic children with mild symptom manifestations can get through this phase relatively easily (Soetjiningsih, 2013).

When children with ASD grow into adults, the work environment for autistic adults can work with proper guidance. However, in reality, many jobs do not accept people with ASD because of their specialties and the communication difficulties they experience (Soetjiningsih, 2013).

C. Unique Traits of Autism in Girls and Women

The clinical manifestations of ASD in boys and girls are slightly different. Girls have a significantly more camouflage mechanism of autism symptoms than boys. This causes a delay in the diagnosis of ASD in girls because the clinical manifestations are unclear. The mechanism of camouflage is caused by the social pressure received by girls to conform to gender roles. On the other hand, girls also have better camouflage strategies because girls are more social (Schuck et al., 2019).

In addition, the symptoms and behavioral patterns between girls and boys are also different. Boys show more repetitive and limited behavior and tend to have more social communication problems than girls due to the camouflage mechanism (Milner et al., 2019).

The clinical implications obtained are that girls with ASD are often undiagnosed or diagnosed late due to the camouflage mechanism which causes symptoms to become more subtle. In addition, girls are also more likely to experience social pressure due to greater social demands which result in more severe psychological problems. Thus, these differences indicate the importance of a more sensitive diagnostic and support approach for women (Milner et al., 2019).

D. Co-occurring Condition : Anxiety, ADHD, and more

Co-occurring or diseases that occur together with ASD can be psychiatric, medical, and neurological conditions that cause complex and expensive diagnosis and management. Some other diseases that often co-occur with ASD are ADHD, followed by anxiety disorders, sleep-wake disorders, disruptive/impulse control disorders, depressive disorders, obsessive-compulsive disorders, bipolar disorders, and schizophrenia spectrum disorders (Micai et al., 2023).

Attention deficit hyperactivity disorder (ADHD)

Children with symptoms of ADHD and ASD diagnosis have higher symptoms of inattention, as well as hyperactive/impulsivity symptoms which are distinguishing symptoms between children diagnosed with ASD only and children diagnosed with ASD and ADHD. The presence of ADHD symptoms in children with ASD is likely to worsen existing ASD symptoms in the form of greater executive function deterioration and more significant emotional deficits. So in other words, children with ASD accompanied by ADHD have additional symptoms of inattention, hyperactivity and impulsivity which worsen the child's condition (Micai et al., 2023).

Anxiety disorder

In ASD, there is an event of insistence on sameness which is one of the behaviors of children with ASD that requires them to follow a fixed routine so that the child has difficulty adapting to change. This behavior can trigger anxiety in children with ASD (Baribeau et al., 2020).

Sleep disorder

The most common sleep disorder is insomnia, both in initiating sleep and maintaining sleep. These sleep problems are related to psychopathology and structural and functional disorders of the neuronal system of ASD in the form of increased orexinergic systems, decreased melatonergic systems, and decreased REM (Petti et al., 2023).

Depressive disorder

Individuals with ASD exhibit more atypical depressive symptoms that focus on special interest involvement, repetitive behaviors, and decreased daily living activities. In addition, some depressive symptoms can overlap with ASD symptoms such as: social isolation, concentration problems, sleep disturbances, and eating disorders.

Obsessive-compulsive disorder

Obsessive compulsive disorder and ASD often occur together, making it challenging to diagnose and manage. Adolescents with OCD + ASD have lower psychosocial functioning scores, so therapy requires a regimen that is more than just being diagnosed with one of these disorders (Martin et al., 2020).

References

Almsmary, S., Waala Alwarfaly, Selima Muftah, Ashmisa Eltuhami, Alsaeti, Z. A., Mansour, R. M., & Ali Ateia Elmabsout. (2022). Childhood Autism: Clinical Characteristics, Nutritional Status, and Psychosocial Features. *Childhood Autism: Clinical Characteristics, Nutritional Status, and Psychosocial Features, 4*(3), 98–104. https://doi.org/10.24018/ejmed.2022.4.3.1156

Baribeau, D. A., Vigod, S., Pullenayegum, E., Kerns, C. M., Mirenda, P., Smith, I. M., Vaillancourt, T., Volden, J., Waddell, C., Zwaigenbaum, L., Bennett, T., Duku, E., Elsabbagh, M., Georgiades, S., Ungar, W. J., Zaidman Zait, A., & Szatmari, P. (2020). Co-occurring trajectories of anxiety and insistence on sameness behaviour in autism spectrum disorder. *The British Journal of Psychiatry, 218*(1), 20–27. https://doi.org/10.1192/bjp.2020.127

Departemen Psikiatri FKUI. (2017). *Buku Ajar Psikiatri*. Edisi Ketiga. Jakarta: Fakultas Kedokteran Universitas Indonesia.

Eckerd, M. (2020). Detection and Diagnosis of ASD in Females. *Journal of Health Service Psychology*, *46*(1), 37–47. https://doi.org/10.1007/s42843-020-00006-1

J. Wolff, J., & Piven, J. (2020). Predicting Autism in Infancy. *Journal of the American Academy of Child & Adolescent Psychiatry*. https://doi.org/10.1016/j.jaac.2020.07.910

Martin, A. F., Jassi, A., Cullen, A. E., Broadbent, M., Downs, J., & Krebs, G. (2020). Co-occurring obsessive–compulsive disorder and autism spectrum disorder in young people: prevalence, clinical characteristics and outcomes. *European Child & Adolescent Psychiatry*, *29*(11), 1603–1611. https://doi.org/10.1007/s00787-020-01478-8

Mash, E. J., Barkley, R. A., & Proquest (Firm. (2014). *Child psychopathology*. The Guilford Press.

Micai, M., Laura Maria Fatta, Letizia Gila, Caruso, A., Salvitti, T., Fulceri, F., Ciaramella, A., D'Amico, R., Cinzia Del Giovane, Bertelli, M. O., Romano, G., Schünemann, H. J., & María Luisa Scattoni. (2023). Prevalence of co-occurring conditions in children and adults with autism spectrum disorder: A systematic review and meta-analysis. *Neuroscience & Biobehavioral Reviews*, *155*, 105436–105436. https://doi.org/10.1016/j.neubiorev.2023.105436

Milner, V., McIntosh, H., Colvert, E., & Happé, F. (2019). A Qualitative Exploration of the Female Experience of Autism Spectrum Disorder (ASD). *Journal of Autism and Developmental Disorders*, *49*(6). https://doi.org/10.1007/s10803-019-03906-4

Petti, T. A., Gupta, M., Fradkin, Y., & Gupta, N. (2023). Management of sleep disorders in autism spectrum disorder with co-occurring attention-deficit hyperactivity disorder: update for clinicians. *British Journal of Psychiatry Open, 10*(1). https://doi.org/10.1192/bjo.2023.589

Posar, A., & Visconti, P. (2022). Early Motor Signs in Autism Spectrum Disorder. *Children, 9*(2), 294. https://doi.org/10.3390/children9020294

Rantalainen, K., Paavola-Ruotsalainen, L., Alakortes, J., Carter, A. S., Ebeling, H. E., & Kunnari, S. (2021). Early vocabulary development: Relationships with prelinguistic skills and early social-emotional/behavioral problems and competencies. *Infant Behavior and Development, 62,* 101525. https://doi.org/10.1016/j.infbeh.2020.101525

Schuck, R. K., Flores, R. E., & Fung, L. K. (2019). Brief Report: Sex/Gender Differences in Symptomology and Camouflaging in Adults with Autism Spectrum Disorder. *Journal of Autism and Developmental Disorders, 49*(6), 2597–2604. https://doi.org/10.1007/s10803-019-03998-y

Soetjiningsih, & Ranuh, I. G. N. (2013). *Tumbuh Kembang Anak* (Edisi ke-2). Jakarta: Penerbit EGC.

Turki Abualait, Alabbad, M., Kaleem, I., Imran, H., Khan, H., Mubin Mustafa Kiyani, & Bashir, S. (2024). Autism Spectrum Disorder in Children: Early Signs and Therapeutic Interventions. *Children, 11*(11), 1311–1311. https://doi.org/10.3390/children11111311.

CHAPTER 4: DIAGNOSING AUTISM SPECTRUM DISORDER

Nabila Az-zahra Hasibuan, Department of Medicine, Faculty of Medicine, Sriwijaya University

A. The Diagnostic Process: From Concerns to Confirmation (ASD)

A diagnosis of Autism Spectrum Disorder (ASD) can be made at any age but is most common in early childhood. Although there is no universal screening instrument, public health systems in various countries in Europe identify children with suspicion of ASD, specifically ages 18-30 months using the M-CHAT (Modified Checklist for Autism in Toddlers) and similar tools such as the Autism Diagnostic Observation Schedule (ADOS) and the Autism Diagnostic Interview Revised (ADI-R). In addition, other screening tools that can be used to assess ASD symptoms in children are the Social Communication Questionnaire (SCQ), Social Responsiveness Scale (SRS), and Childhood Autism Rating Scale (CARS) (Lordan, 2021).

The gold standard of ASD diagnosis with high sensitivity and specificity is the Autism Diagnostic Observation Schedule (ADOS), based on professional observations in several settings, and parent interviews using the Autism Diagnostic Interview-Revised (ADI-R) (Hus *and* Segal, 2021).

According to Soetjiningsih (2015), a valid and reliable diagnosis of ASD is made with many sources including observations from the clinician, information from caregivers, and if possible from the patient's own report. The diagnosis of ASD should be made with a comprehensive evaluation based on three main issues, namely:
1. Determine the overall function of the child
2. Determine the ASD diagnosis category
3. Determine the presence of other underlying diseases.

A comprehensive evaluation of ASD consists of several components namely:
1. Health, development and behavioral history in pedigree form for at least 3 generations
2. Detailed physical examination consisting of dysmorphic features, neurological abnormalities
3. Developmental evaluation and psychometrics
4. Determine if the child has ASD according to DSM-5 criteria
5. Assessment of parental knowledge and skills
6. Laboratory examination (still contraindicated)

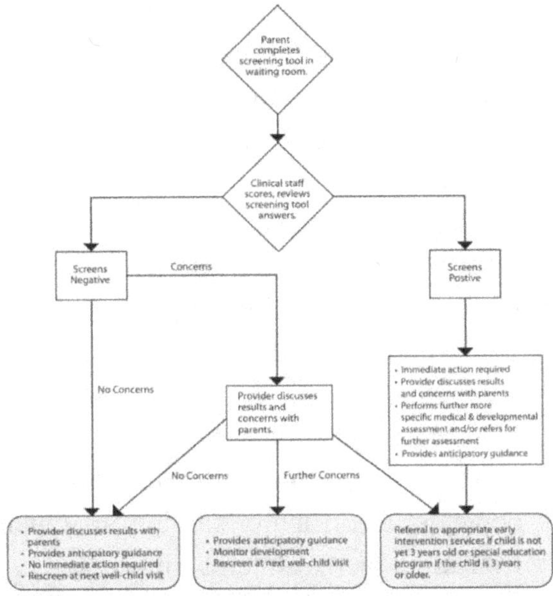

Figure 4.1. Flowchart of pediatric developmental screening (Okoye et al., 2023)

B. Common Diagnostic Tools and Tests (ASD)

Autism Spectrum Disorder (ASD) is a clinical diagnosis so that diagnosis is made based on careful clinical observation and interviews with parents/caregivers regarding the child's developmental history. The primary diagnostic tool in Autism Spectrum Disorder (ASD) is done by evaluating the suitability of the patient's condition with DSM-5 criteria and screening using M-CHAT-R by analyzing "yes/no" responses covering different developmental domains to formulate a diagnosis (Lordan *et al,* 2021).

Diagnostic and Statistical Manual of Mental Disorders, Fifth Edition (DSM-5) (American Psychiatric Association, 2013)

Referring to the DSM-5, the diagnostic criteria in a child suspected of Autism Spectrum Disorder (ASD) should have persistent deficits in each of the three areas of communication and social interaction and a minimum of two of the four restrictive and repetitive behaviors.

a. Deficits in communication and social interaction skills across a range of current contexts and previous developmental history.

    i.   Social-emotional reciprocity deficits that include abnormal social approachability, inability to have two-way conversations, reduced willingness to share interests, emotions or affect, and failure to initiate or respond to social interactions.

    ii.   Nonverbal communicative behavior deficits in social interactions, consisting of unintegrated verbal and nonverbal communication, abnormalities in eye contact and body language, and lack of facial expressions and nonverbal communication.

    iii.   Deficits in the ability to develop, maintain, and understand relationships, from difficulty adjusting behavior to social contexts, to difficulty sharing imaginative play or making friends, to lack of interest in peers.

b. Restrictive and repetitive patterns of behavior seen in the present or in the past.

    i.   Motor movements, repetitive use of objects or speech

    ii.   A tendency to do uniform things, inflexibility to routines, or repetitive patterns of behavior.

    iii.   Very limited and intensity-dependent interests or abnormal focus

    iv.   Hyper- or hypo-reactivity to sensory impulses or unusual interest in sensory aspects of the environment

c. Symptoms of ASD should be visible from early developmental periods, but may still go undetected

d. The symptoms cause clinically significant impairment in social, occupational, or other important areas of current functioning.

e. This disorder cannot be better explained by intellectual developmental disorder (intellectual disability) or global developmental delay.

Modified Checklist for Autism in Toddlers, Revised with Follow Up (M-CHAT-R/F)

M-CHAT-R/F is a screening tool to detect the risk level of Autism Spectrum Disorder in children aged 16-30 months. The M-CHAT-R aims to detect as many cases of ASD as possible in less than 2 minutes. However, the use of M-CHAT-R is prone to false-positive results as it can indicate the risk of other developmental delays, so it is necessary to follow up using M-CHAT-F based on which questions the child failed on M-CHAT-R. If the M-CHAT-R/F result shows a positive result, it is recommended to refer the child for early intervention or diagnostic testing as soon as possible (Robins *et al,* 2009).

Autism Diagnostic Interview Revised (ADI-R)

The ADI-R is a semi-structured interview applied by a trained examiner to relatives and/or caregivers to collect information regarding development in the first years of a patient's life based on everyday behaviors and skills (Frigaux *et al,* 2019). The ADI-R focuses on systematic and standardized observations of behaviors rarely found in non-clinical subjects, and mainly on three areas of functioning, namely language and communication, shared social interactions, stereotyped behaviors, and restricted interests (Perinelli *and* Cloherty, 2023).

A Diagnostic Observation Schedule, Second Edition (ADOS-2)

The Autism diagnostic observation schedule or ADOS is a tool used to help clinicians assess autism in children, adolescents, and adults using games and conversations with the aim of eliciting information from the child or adolescent. The ADOS consists of four modules that include specific items that are combined into a diagnostic algorithm with module-specific cutoff scores for autism and autism spectrum versus non-ASD. ADOS assessment aspects consist of communication skills, social skills, play skills, restricted and repetitive behaviors and other abnormal behaviors, such as hyperactivity, disruptive behaviors, and anxiety (Hong *et al,* 2022).

Social Communication Questionnaire (SCQ)

The Social Communication Questionnaire (SCQ) is a

screening tool used for the assessment of autism spectrum disorder (ASD) with higher sensitivity and specificity in older children (Hollocks *et al,* 2019).

The SCQ consists of a short screening of 40 questions about children's daily habits that point to symptoms of ASD with yes/no answers and is asked to parents/caregivers. The SCQ consists of 2 types of forms, namely current which is based on the history of the child's habits in the last 3 months and lifetime which is based on the child's overall developmental history. The SCQ is a modified form of the ADI-R designed as a companion tool to other diagnostic methods. The advantages of the SCQ are that it takes less time to complete than the ADI-R and does not require the assistance of a therapist so it can be completed by caregivers. The use of the SCQ serves to screen children for possible autism spectrum disorder. High scores on the SCQ can be followed by diagnostic evaluation using the ADI-R, ADOS and ADI-R in combination with the ADOS (Mulligan *et al,* 2009).

Social Responsiveness Scale (SRS)

The Social Responsiveness Scale is a quantitative measure of autism traits in children and adolescents by assessing history of reciprocal social behavior and social-communicative abilities, including specific items related to ASD and non-specific items in patients with suspected ASD symptoms (Nguyen *et al,* 2019). However, the SRS's 65 items make detection burdensome, so evaluation of this method is recommended in school-aged children rather than pre-school-aged children (Kaat *et al,* 2023).

Childhood Autism Rating Scale (CARS) (Moon et al, 2019)

The Childhood Autism Rating Scale (CARS) is an ASD diagnostic tool discovered in 1980 and updated to CARS-2 in 2010. CARS is a physician assessment questionnaire consisting of 15 items covering social, emotional, adaptive, communicative, and cognitive functioning. The CARS assessment consists of 4 points that are based on individual observations as well as additional information, such as parent and/or teacher reports. The final results of the CARS assessment are divided into three levels, namely:

- Minimal to no ASD symptoms: 15-29.5 in children <13 years of age and 15-27.5 in children >13 years of age
- Mild to moderate ASD symptoms: 30-36.5 in children <13 years of age and 28-34.5 in children >13 years of age
- Severe ASD symptoms: ≥37 in children <13 years of age and ≥35 in children >13 years of age

C. The Role of Early Screening and Intervention

Early diagnosis and intervention in ASD plays a role in improving the well-being of parents to deal with problems and reduce stress so that it can show a good prognosis in children with ASD. Ideally, the diagnosis of ASD is made when symptoms appear before 3 years of age, but sometimes it can be delayed until the child is 6 years of age or older (Abubakar *and* Kipkemoi, 2022).

Diagnosis of developmental disorders at an early age aims to target effective and timely therapy to minimize symptoms so that children can adapt well and are expected to become independent individuals in adulthood. Early diagnosis and intervention conducted before the child is 4 years old (between 12 and 48 months) shows significant improvements in the development of cognition, language, and adaptive behavior (Hus *and* Segal, 2021).

D. Challenges in Diagnosing Autism

A challenge in the early detection of ASD is the weakness in the requirements of current diagnostic criteria and standardized assessment tools, which makes the diagnosis of ASD prone to showing true or false results that do not match the patient's condition. An accurate diagnosis of ASD according to DSM-5 relies on limited social communication impairments and repetitive behaviors that cannot be exaggerated. As a result, children are prone to missed diagnoses or false negative results, resulting in early intervention and delayed treatment. In addition, the similarity of ASD symptoms with other developmental disorders can lead to false positive results that can cause family concern and increased therapy costs that are not necessary. The DSM-5 criteria for ASD are easier to apply in severe cases of ASD, but significantly more difficult to meet in milder conditions of ASD due to less obvious behaviors (Hus *and* Segal, 2021).

References

Abubakar, A., & Kipkemoi, P. (2022). Early intervention in autism spectrum disorder: The need for an international approach. *Developmental Medicine & Child Neurology*, *64*(9), 1051–1058. https://doi.org/10.1111/dmcn.15327

American Psychiatric Association. (2013). *Diagnostic and statistical manual of mental disorders* (5th ed.). American Psychiatric Publishing.

Frigaux, A., Evrard, R., & Lighezzolo-Alnot, J. (2019). ADI-R and ADOS and the Differential Diagnosis of Autism Spectrum disorders: Interests, Limits and Openings. *L'Encéphale*, *45*(5), 441–448. https://doi.org/10.1016/j.encep.2019.07.002

Hollocks, M. J., Casson, R., White, C., Dobson, J., Beazley, P., & Humphrey, A. (2019). Brief Report: An Evaluation of the Social Communication Questionnaire as a Screening Tool for Autism Spectrum Disorder in Young People Referred to Child & Adolescent Mental Health Services. *Journal of Autism and Developmental Disorders*, *49*(6), 2618–2623. https://doi.org/10.1007/s10803-019-03982-6

Hong, J. S., Singh, V., Kalb, L., Reetzke, R., Ludwig, N. N., Pfeiffer, D., Holingue, C., Menon, D., Lu, Q., Ashkar, A., & Landa, R. (2022). Replication study for ADOS-2 cut-offs to assist evaluation of autism spectrum disorder. *Autism Research*, *15*(11), 2181–2191. https://doi.org/10.1002/aur.2801

Hus, Y., & Segal, O. (2021). Challenges Surrounding the Diagnosis of

Autism in Children. *Neuropsychiatric Disease and Treatment*, *17*(17), 3509–3529. https://doi.org/10.2147/NDT.S282569

Kaat, A. J., Croen, L. A., Constantino, J., Newshaffer, C. J., & Lyall, K. (2023). Modifying the social responsiveness scale for adaptive administration. *Quality of Life Research*, *32*(8), 2353–2360. https://doi.org/10.1007/s11136-023-03397-y

Lordan, R., Storni, C., & De Benedictis, C. A. (2021). *Autism Spectrum Disorders: Diagnosis and Treatment* (A. M. Grabrucker, Ed.). PubMed; Exon Publications. https://www.ncbi.nlm.nih.gov/books/NBK573609/

Moon, S. J., Hwang, J. S., Shin, A. L., Kim, J. Y., Bae, S. M., Sheehy-Knight, J., & Kim, J. W. (2019). Accuracy of the Childhood Autism Rating Scale: a systematic review and meta-analysis. *Developmental Medicine & Child Neurology*, *61*(9), 1030–1038. https://doi.org/10.1111/dmcn.14246

Mulligan, A., Richardson, T., Anney, R. J. L., & Gill, M. (2009). The Social Communication Questionnaire in a sample of the general population of school-going children. *Irish Journal of Medical Science*, *178*(2), 193–199. https://doi.org/10.1007/s11845-008-0184-5

Nguyen, P. H., Ocansey, M. E., Miller, M., Le, D. T. K., Schmidt, R. J., & Prado, E. L. (2019). The reliability and validity of the social responsiveness scale to measure autism symptomology in Vietnamese children. *Autism Research*, *12*(11), 1706–1718. https://doi.org/10.1002/aur.2179

Okoye, C., Obialo-Ibeawuchi, C. M., Obajeun, O. A., Sarwar, S., Tawfik, C., Waleed, M. S., Wasim, A. U., Mohamoud, I., Afolayan, A. Y., & Mbaezue, R. N. (2023). Early Diagnosis of Autism Spectrum Disorder: A Review and Analysis of the Risks and Benefits. *Cureus*, *15*(8). https://doi.org/10.7759/cureus.43226

Perinelli, M. G., & Cloherty, M. (2023). Identification of autism in cognitively able adults with epilepsy: A narrative review and discussion of available screening and diagnostic tools. *Seizure, 104*, 6–11. https://doi.org/10.1016/j.seizure.2022.11.004

Robins, D. L., Fein, D., & Barton, M. (2009). *M-CHATTM - Autism Screening*. M-CHATTM. https://www.mchatscreen.com/

Soetjiningsih, Windiani, I. G. A. T., & Adnyana, I. G. A. N. S. (2015). *Pedoman Pelatihan Deteksi Dini dan Diagnosis Gangguan Spektrum Autisme (ASD)*. Ilmu Kesehatan Anak FK UNUD-Sangla.

CHAPTER 5: INTERVENTIONS AND THERAPIES FOR AUTISM

Dyah Fatha Istiqomah, Department of Medicine, Faculty of Medicine, Sriwijaya University

A. Evidence-Based Behavioral Interventions

For many years, applied behavior analysis (ABA) and interventions developed from its principles have been empirically studied and clinically applied for autistic individuals diagnosed with autism spectrum disorder (ASD). ABA is the practice of utilizing psychological principles of learning theory to effect changes in behaviors commonly seen in individuals diagnosed with ASD at all levels of functioning, including cognition, language, social skills, problem behaviors, and daily living skills. This methodology is highly effective in teaching basic communication, play, exercise, social interaction, daily living, and self-help skills. One well-known and often-cited basic model is the "antecedents, behaviors, and consequences," otherwise known as the ABC model, in which manipulating both the antecedents and consequences of behavior is intended to increase, decrease, or modify the behavior, resulting in a transferable tool for effectively targeting desired behaviors (Gitimoghaddam et al., 2022).

Currently, there are several types of interventions that are based on ABA and share a set of core features. Comprehensive ABA-based treatment models have intervention targets that cover all aspects of functioning, such as independent living skills, social skills, motor skills, pre-academic and academic skills, and language. Some specific comprehensive ABA-based treatment models:

Early intensive behavioral intervention (EIBI)

EIBI is intended for children under the age of 5 years and is usually provided between 20 and 40 hours per week for several consecutive years. The program is delivered individually (one-on-one) in a structured environment, such as at home or school, often using discrete conversational training (DTT) methods and combined with other more flexible teaching methods, such as natural environment-based training (Gitimoghaddam et al., 2022).

Early Start Denver Model (ESDM)

ESDM is designed for children with ASD aged 12 to 60 months. This intervention combines naturalistic teaching methods in ABA with the goal of providing a comprehensive, developmentally based, and early relationship-focused behavioral approach (Gitimoghaddam et al., 2022). ESDM emphasizes teaching strategies that involve positive social interactions, participation in real-life activities, and adult responsiveness to the child's cues, and it emphasizes verbal and nonverbal communication, based on a curriculum that addresses all aspects of development (Yu et al., 2020).

Learning Experiences: An Alternative Program for Preschoolers and Their Parents (LEAP)

LEAP is a model implemented in a public school setting and developed based on the basic principles of ABA. The model includes a variety of methods commonly used in ABA, such as Pivotal Response Training (PRT), time delay, incidental teaching, peer-involved interventions, and PECS. Central to LEAP is an emphasis on parent and peer involvement in behavioral teaching strategies, utilizing naturally occurring incidental teaching, as opposed to the more structured, adult-led approach used in many other ABA strategies (Gitimoghaddam et al., 2022).

Discrete Trial Training (DTT)

DTT is a basic intervention method in ABA that involves a series of instructions and repetitions in one-on-one sessions without interruption. The main focus of DTT is to teach new behaviors, both consciously and unconsciously, to the child (Gitimoghaddam et al., 2022). This method consists of direct and systematic instructions that are repeated until the child masters the skill, by breaking the skill down into small elements for analysis (Yu et al., 2020).

Pivotal Response Treatment (PRT)

PRT aims to increase children's initiative and motivation to communicate effectively in everyday life contexts (Gitimoghaddam et al., 2022). This intervention focuses on setting up an environment that supports the use of target communication structures and then providing opportunities for children to use these structures in natural play interactions (Yu et al., 2020).

Picture Exchange Communication Systems (PECS)

PECS is a manualized program that guides children to use an exchange-based communication system, which has become a common intervention option for nonverbal children with ASD in clinical and school settings (Yu et al., 2020).

Functional Communication Training (FCT)

FCT, a differential reinforcement-based procedure, reduces problem behaviors by replacing them with more appropriate communicative responses. This training is commonly used in conjunction with other ABA methods (Gitimoghaddam et al., 2022).

Although these interventions have their own designs and forms of performance, they are all consistent with the principles of ABA and have shown effectiveness in different functions of children with ASD (Yu et al., 2020).

Based on the journal (Gitimoghaddam et al., 2022) it was found that ABA programs for children with ASD resulted in moderate to highly effective improvements in expressive and receptive language skills, communication skills, nonverbal IQ scores, total adaptive behavior, and socialization, but less improvement in daily living skills. According to the US Department of Health and Human Services (1999), ABA is the gold standard treatment for ASD. However, the lack of information regarding the subject's Quality of Life measures makes continued research and development of the SoC necessary. All interventions for children and adolescents with ASD must be held to existing standards set by ABA to be considered effective until the SoC is established.

B. Speech and Occupational Therapy for Autism

At initial presentation, many individuals with autism spectrum disorder have intellectual and/or language impairments (e.g., late speech, language comprehension lagging behind production) that are often accompanied by a lack of social interest or social interaction and unusual communication patterns. Deafness may be suspected but is usually ruled out. Those with average or high intelligence also typically have an uneven ability profile due to the often large gap between intellectual and adaptive functional skills. It is common for individuals with autism to have theory of mind deficits (i.e., having difficulty seeing the world from another person's perspective), although this is not always present in all cases. Executive function deficits are also common but not specific, as are difficulties with central coherence (i.e., being able to understand context or "see the big picture," and thus tending to focus too much on details) (American Psychiatric Association, 2022).

According to (Vogindroukas et al., 2022), the growing body of longitudinal research evidence of young children with and without ASD suggests that those with impairments in verbal skills are at higher risk for poor outcomes later in life. Early language skills and their development predict social functioning, academic achievement, and psychiatric outcomes in late childhood and adulthood. The influence of social development is an important cause of language and speech difficulties in children with ASD.

Different language profiles in ASD will help guide appropriate intervention programs. Based on the journal (Vogindroukas et al., 2022), the categorization of different language profiles in ASD can be arranged into 4 types:

- Type 1: ASD with pragmatic language impairment without other language difficulties. Difficulties in the development of pragmatic language are associated with manifestations of difficulties in social functioning, and are not an element of developmental language disorder and/or comorbidity. This group also includes individuals with very good and exceptional language abilities, but who have difficulties in so-called functional language, and/or non-verbal behaviors related to communication, and who will only have difficulties using language for social needs.

- Type 2: ASD accompanied by DLD and other developmental disorders such as SSD, or/and AS. These children will show impairments in social functioning and stereotyped behaviors along with impairments in language and speech development.

- Type 3: ASD accompanied by intellectual disability with global delays in language and general intelligence. IQ has a strong influence on language development in children with ASD and most children who do not develop the ability to speak phrases also have a nonverbal IQ below 70.

- Type 4: ASD with severe difficulties in the development of social communication and social interaction and secondary language difficulties as a result of the non-use of language as a means of communication.

In the first type of the above categorization of ASD with language pragmatic disorders without other language disorders, interventions will focus on understanding social situations, direct use of language in social communication, understanding the social aspects of language and their inclusion in real-life situations, understanding figurative language, and socially based language constructions. However, in the latter type, early intervention for language and speech development will have a key role in preventing the development of this type of difficulty. Since parental language input will influence language and speech development in the first years of a child's life, a strong intervention option in this category is a parenting program that targets the early development of language, communication, and social skills (Vogindroukas et al., 2022).

According to (American Psychiatric Association, 2022), children with ASD have extreme difficulties in planning, organizing, and coping with change that negatively impact academic achievement, even for students with above-average intelligence. Occupational therapists can help people with autism to recognize, acknowledge, and support their strengths and to advocate for the use of these strengths as assets in settings such as school and work (Kirby et al., 2023).

Occupational therapists play a critical role because they intervene directly in the autonomy and independence of children and adolescents with ASD in a variety of settings, such as home and school. These professionals use meaningful work and activities; in this population, this can be play, in a structured way as a means of rehabilitation, and they develop interventions with the preferences, needs, and abilities of people with ASD in mind (Domínguez-Lucio et al., 2022).

In particular, scientific evidence on occupational therapy (OT) interventions using new technologies (NT) in children and adolescents with ASD has shown beneficial effects on children's academic skills (literacy and numeracy), performance of daily living activities, and acquisition of social skills (interaction and collaboration with peers) (Domínguez-Lucio et al., 2022).

C. Educational Approaches and Individualized Learning Plans

The need for effective services and strategies to support the transition from school to post-school/work experiences for individuals with disabilities and specifically autism spectrum disorder (ASD) is increasing. After-school options are limited, and most adults with

ASD struggle to find adequate and stable employment opportunities (Laghi & Trimarco, 2020).

A carefully designed Individual Learning Plan provides opportunities for children with ASD to learn in the way that best suits them. In the journal (Laghi & Trimarco, 2020), it is shown that individualized educational planning (IEP) is an expression of the right to education for people with disabilities. The IEP identifies tools, strategies, and methods to achieve an optimal learning environment in the following dimensions: relationships, socialization, communication, interaction, orientation, and autonomy. The IEP also contains educational and evaluation methods related to the individual program and defines tools for the actual realization of the "alternating school-work system." The IEP is jointly developed, according to the individual's functional profile, by the student's classroom teacher, family, and specific professional figures inside and outside the school. The school is formally integrated as part of the individual's life project, which supports the life course perspective.

There are two main points that can play an important role in promoting independent living and supporting the transition to the world of work based on the journal (Laghi & Trimarco, 2020), namely:

1. Integration of the IEP into a broader individual project can facilitate the planning of skills that will be needed in the work environment and should be developed starting from the school stage.

2. The definition of specific and individual strategies and tools for the success of the alternating school-work system, included in the IEP, can allow early contact with the work context.

The educational approach for children with autism should be flexible, structured and based on the child's strengths and needs. An example of a structured approach is the TEACCH (Treatment and Education of Autistic and Communication-Handicapped Children) technique. The TEACCH Transition Assessment Profile (TTAP) is used to evaluate the ability to plan the transition from school age to adolescence and adulthood. The TTAP test items cover six functional areas of vocational skills, vocational behavior, independent functioning, leisure skills, functional communication, and interpersonal behavior, with observations of student performance in several tasks, and with interviews for teachers and parents to evaluate abilities related to the school and family context. For each ability, it is possible to evaluate the student's performance on a 3-point scale P (pass), E (improving), or F (fail) (Laghi & Trimarco, 2020).

The child's progress can also be monitored periodically to assess its effectiveness. Objective monitoring can also be considered a critical point: teachers who are not used to being observed, for example through video units, sometimes experience observation as a test rather than a way to think about the process with the consultant (Laghi & Trimarco, 2020).

Training for teachers on targeted intervention practices and autism is critical, as support teachers may not have received specific training on ASD and may not be experienced in working with individuals with this condition. According to the journal (Love et al., 2019), teachers who believe they can teach students with ASD are also more likely to engage positively with their students with ASD and have higher levels of achievement of their students' IEP goals. Key elements associated with real-life projects and favorable transition outcomes according to the journal (Laghi & Trimarco, 2020), include:

1. Parent and teacher involvement is critical in evaluating the strengths, challenges, and transition outcomes of students with ASD. Parents support the development of lifelong skills, while teachers teach skills and learning goals. Under the COMPASS model, parents and teachers engage in an initial consultation to design individual goals and a tailored instructional plan. Parents and students (if applicable) also provide input regarding post-school goals. Following the consultation, the consultant meets again with parents,

teachers, and students in several sessions to evaluate progress and strategies. Collaborative problem solving is also an important part of this model. Internship programs in high schools can help students with ASD develop job skills, increasing their chances for success in the adult workforce.

2. Peer strengths (PMIs), which are their ability to assist students with ASD in the general education setting, especially if they are trained as peers. With structured procedures and proper training, the school environment can be a supportive place for positive social interactions for adolescents with ASD.

3. Parent involvement in building the future of their son or daughter with special needs.

D. Alternative Therapies: What Works and What Doesn't

Many therapies have been studied in recent years. There are therapies that have been proven effective; that is, they have been supported by many scientific studies and have been shown to provide real benefits for many children with ASD, such as ABA, speech therapy, occupational therapy, and social skills training. On the other hand, there are also therapies that are more controversial or not supported by strong scientific evidence; that is, they do not show significant benefits and can be risky if applied without proper supervision. Controversial or unproven therapies include:

Gluten-free and casein-free [GFCF] diet

A gluten-free and casein-free [GFCF] diet is an elimination diet that involves eliminating certain proteins from the normal diet, such as gluten and casein. However, there is no strong evidence to show the benefits of a GFCF diet in patients with ASD (Baspinar & Yardimci, 2020).

Chelation therapy (heavy metal removal)

There is no clinical trial evidence to show that chelation therapy is an effective intervention for ASD. In addition, this therapy can cause serious side effects, such as hypocalcemia, kidney disorders, and reported deaths; the risks of using chelation for ASD currently outweigh the proven benefits (James et al., 2015).

Hyperbaric Oxygen Therapy

Hyperbaric oxygen therapy (HBOT) was initially suggested as an effective therapy method in ASD, but several studies have shown that it is not recommended to use this form of therapy in children with ASD, and no studies have shown that HBOT is effective in cases of ASD (Podgórska-Bednarz & Perenc, 2021).

Doman-Delacato Therapy (Patterning Therapy)

This therapy aims to stimulate the neurological development of children with developmental disorders through a series of movement patterns and physical exercises designed to "reprogram" the child's brain, but there is no strong enough scientific evidence to show that it is effective in treating autism or other developmental disorders (Cummins, 2018).

Music therapy

Music therapy may be associated with increased chances of global improvement for people with autism, but there is no clear evidence of differences for social interaction, nonverbal communication, and verbal communication measured immediately after the intervention (Geretsegger et al., 2022).

References

American Psychiatric Association. (2022). *Diagnostic and statistical manual of mental disorders* (5th ed.). American Psychiatric Publishing.

Baspinar, B., & Yardimci, H. (2020). Is Gluten-Free Casein-Free Diet Effective in Resolving Gastrointestinal Problems and Behaviors in Autism Spectrum Disorder. *The Eurasian of Medicine, 52*(3). https://doi.org/10.5152/eurasianjmed.2020.19230

Cummins, R. A. (2018). The Neurologically Impaired Child.

In *Routledge eBooks*. Informa. https://doi.org/10.4324/9780429490163

Domínguez-Lucio, S., Compañ-Gabucio, L. M., Torres-Collado, L., & de la Hera, M. G. (2022). Occupational Therapy Interventions Using New Technologies in Children and Adolescents with Autism Spectrum Disorder: A Scoping Review. *Journal of Autism and Developmental Disorders*, *53*(1), 332–358. https://doi.org/10.1007/s10803-022-05431-3

Geretsegger, M., Fusar-Poli, L., Elefant, C., Mössler, K. A., Vitale, G., & Gold, C. (2022). Music therapy for autistic people. *Cochrane Database of Systematic Reviews*, *2022*(5). https://doi.org/10.1002/14651858.cd004381.pub4

Gitimoghaddam, M., Chichkine, N., McArthur, L., Sangha, S. S., & Symington, V. (2022). Applied Behavior Analysis in Children and Youth with Autism Spectrum Disorders: A Scoping Review. *Perspectives on Behavior Science*, *45*(3). https://doi.org/10.1007/s40614-022-00338-x

James, S., Stevenson, S. W., Silove, N., & Williams, K. (2015). Chelation for autism spectrum disorder (ASD). *Cochrane Database of Systematic Reviews*. https://doi.org/10.1002/14651858.cd010766.pub2

Kirby, A. V., Morgan, L., & Hilton, C. (2023). Autism and Mental Health: The Role of Occupational Therapy. *American Journal of Occupational Therapy*, *77*(2), 1–4. https://doi.org/10.5014/ajot.2023.050303

Laghi, F., & Trimarco, B. (2020). Individual planning starts at school. Tools and practices promoting autonomy and supporting transition to work for adolescents with autism spectrum disorder. *Ann Ist Super Sanità*, *56*(2), 222–229. https://doi.org/10.4415/ANN_20_02_12

Love, A. M. A., Findley, J. A., Ruble, L. A., & McGrew, J. H. (2019). Teacher Self-Efficacy for Teaching Students with Autism Spectrum Disorder: Associations with Stress, Teacher

Engagement, and Student IEP Outcomes Following COMPASS Consultation. *Focus on Autism and Other Developmental Disabilities, 35*(1), 108835761983676. https://doi.org/10.1177/1088357619836767

Podgórska-Bednarz, J., & Perenc, L. (2021). Hyperbaric Oxygen Therapy for Children and Youth with Autism Spectrum Disorder: A Review. *Brain Sciences, 11*(7), 916. https://doi.org/10.3390/brainsci11070916

Vogindroukas, I., Stankova, M., Chelas, E.-N., & Proedrou, A. (2022). Language and Speech Characteristics in Autism. *Neuropsychiatric Disease and Treatment, 18,* 2367–2377. https://doi.org/10.2147/ndt.s331987

Yu, Q., Li, E., Li, L., & Liang, W. (2020). Efficacy of Interventions Based on Applied Behavior Analysis for Autism Spectrum Disorder: a Meta-Analysis. *Psychiatry Investigation, 17*(5), 432–443.https://doi.org/10.30773/pi.2019.0229

CHAPTER 6: LIVING WITH AUTISM

Putri Salsabillah, Department of Medicine, Faculty of Medicine, Sriwijaya University

A. Daily Challenges and Strengths of Individuals with Autism

Challenges

> Inherent 'differences' limit potentialities

Some of the unique differences in people with ASD in responding are largely incomprehensible to others and or largely misunderstood. People with ASD also have difficulties in processing such as following instructions, understanding emotions, socializing and interacting appropriately (Halder et al., 2022).

> Limited, need-based alternative support system in schools

Parents of children with ASD feel that children with ASD need a positive, comfortable and supportive environment. Parents also complain that this is also exacerbated by the lack of alternative teaching-learning approaches by teachers in the classroom and school environment, where there is a lack of teacher knowledge, awareness and orientation towards ASD children (Halder et al., 2022).

➢ Striving to fit in undermines mental health

Most of the general public has anxiety about people with ASD. As such, some parents of children with ASD often try to help their children adjust to their environment, both with people with ASD and normal people in general, which can trigger the mental health of children with ASD (Halder et al., 2022).

➢ Complexities understanding individual needs

Some parents of people with ASD feel that school personnel lack the time, effort and willingness to understand individual needs, such as understanding the source of problems that exacerbate struggles and impede learning (Halder et al., 2022).

➢ Camouflaging in girls and the resulting delays in diagnosis and intervention

Some girls with ASD can behave like normal people, such as making good eye contact, developing normally, being considered gifted and not showing repetitive behaviors but have difficulties in understanding spatial issues, sarcasm, tone of voice, humor and emotions. This can result in delayed diagnosis and traumatic experiences in social contexts, so they are not appropriately supported at home or school (Halder et al., 2022).

➢ Communication Barriers

Children with ASD often struggle with communication and have limited verbal skills (Bravata et al., 2020).

➢ The Role of Families and Caregivers

ASD can affect families by causing high levels of stress,

depression and stigma (Bravata et al., 2020).

➢ Sleep Disorders in ASD

Sleep disturbances are found in 70%-75% of children with ASD and 45%-50% of healthy children. Lack of sleep can lead to poor attention, memory, learning and impaired behavior (Bravata et al., 2020).

Strengths

➢ Artistic and/or creative traits

Most children with ASD are especially gifted in the area of creativity where they show their talents in drawing and painting (Halder et al., 2022).

➢ Exceptional faculty of memory

Many people with ASD have exceptional memory skills. Some of them can also remember and then identify directly with related things (Halder et al., 2022).

➢ Mathematical aptitude

Some children with ASD have above-average math skills, such as in a study where a second-grader with ASD could understand higher-level math in fourth grade (Halder et al., 2022).

➢ Musical ability

Many children with ASD have unique musical abilities. They show a high sensitivity to music that can support their development and can express themselves freely (Halder et al., 2022).

➢ Heightened visual perception and attention to detail

ASD children tend to focus on small things or details and they are faster at recognizing objects, shapes or colors. ASD children also have abilities such as putting together puzzles or building structures with blocks (Halder et al., 2022).

B. Understanding Sensory Sensitivities

Individuals with Autism Spectrum Disorder (ASD) often have unique sensory sensitivities. There is hyper- or hyporeactivity to sensory input or unusual interest in sensory aspects of the environment in children with ASD, such as indifference to pain or temperature, poor response to certain sounds or textures, excessive smelling or touching of objects, excessive visual interest in light or movement (American Psychiatric Association, 2022).

- ➢ Hypersensitivity
  - ○ Visual

    People with ASD tend to dislike bright lights, flashing lights or patterns that make the eyes feel uncomfortable (MARCO et al., 2012).

  - ○ Auditory

    People with ASD feel that sounds such as music, vehicle noise, people talking make them uncomfortable and feel disturbed or even painful. Excessive noise can cause anxiety and emotions in people with ASD (MARCO et al., 2012).

  - ○ Tactile

    People with ASD are sensitive to touch, for example, textures such as fabric on clothing, being touched by people, nudging something that provides touch and stimulation to certain areas suddenly can cause discomfort and anxiety (MARCO et al., 2012).

- ➢ Hyposensitivity
  - ○ Visual

    Some people with ASD feel more comfortable when in places or rooms that have dimmer or darker lighting, as bright light can interfere with their vision (MARCO et al., 2012).

  - ○ Auditory

    Some people with ASD find it normal or even

unresponsive to sounds that others find loud and disturbing, and some even seek out environments with noise (MARCO et al., 2012).

o Tactile

Some people with ASD may be less or even unaware of pain, temperature like others (MARCO et al., 2012).

C. Building Communication Skills: Verbal and Non-Verbal

Children with ASD (Austism Spectrum Disorder) experience difficulties in communication and have limited verbal and non-verbal skills. Many things can be done to improve communication skills related to ASD. Creating a supportive environment is essential to encourage communication (Bravata et al., 2020).

Augmentative and alternative communication (AAC) consists of all forms of non-verbal communication, including sign language, picture symbols, gestures, and sound generating devices. AAC has the disadvantage that it cannot provide opportunities for children to communicate verbally independently. This method is best used to gain the child's trust (Bravata et al., 2020).

Opportunities to Initiate Communication (OTI) car a involves manipulating the environment, violating the child's expectations, or other approaches that encourage the student to initiate communication. An example is giving a child a juice box without a straw, this forces the child to use communication skills and ask for the straw independently (Bravata et al., 2020).

Opportunities to Respond (OTR) not only improves student communication but also increases student engagement, improves achievement and learning, and reduces problem behaviors. An example of OTR is asking a child how he or she is currently feeling and waiting for an appropriate response (Bravata et al., 2020).

As individuals with ASD lack communication skills, it is difficult to understand or describe their feelings and emotions. People living with this incurable disorder often experience vulnerability to mental health issues such as anxiety and depression. Understanding feelings enables survival, attachment, interaction, and growth, but for individuals with ASD, it is more beneficial to ask what is important to them than to ask what is a problem (Bravata et al., 2020).

References

American Psychiatric Association. (2022). *Diagnostic and Statistical Manual of Mental Disorders* (5th-TR). American Psychiatric Association.

Bravata, T. M., Kegeler, K. M., Sage, T. J., & Abraham, S. P. (2020). *Living with Autism: Challenges and Resources. Living with Autism: Challenges and Resources*, 17(2), 106 119. https://www.researchgate.net/publication/348391008

Halder, S., Bruyere, S. M., & Gower, W. S. (2022). *Understanding strengths and challenges of people with autism: insights from parents and practitioners. International Journal of Developmental Disabilities*, 70(1), 1–15. https://doi.org/10.1080/20473869.2022.2058781

MARCO, E. J., HINKLEY, L. B. N., HILL, S. S., & NAGARAJAN, S. S. (2012). *Sensory Processing in Autism: A Review of Neurophysiologic Findings. Pediatric Research*, 69(5 Part 2), 48–54. https://doi.org/10.1203/pdr.0b013e3182130c54

CHAPTER 7: THE ROLE OF FAMILIES AND CAREGIVERS

Muhammad Valdis Muyassar, Department of Medicine, Faculty of Medicine, Sriwijaya University

A. Parenting a Child with Autism: Strategies and Support

Children with autism need attention and support from their surroundings. The most important support comes from parents. Parents must be able to provide full support to their children with autism. Here are steps that parents can take to educate children with autism.

Understand autism

Before providing education to children with autism, parents must understand what autism is. A deep understanding of the condition experienced by the child will lead to feelings of compassion and love for the child. These feelings will make parents more patient in dealing with their child's unusual behavior (Bradshaw et al., 2022).

Create a supportive environment

Children with autism need support from the environment in which they live. Make sure the people around him are people who understand his situation and want to help him (O'Nions et al., 2020).

Create a routine

Daily routines will familiarize your child with the environment he is in. Without a routine, children with autism will find it difficult to interact with the environment because they are faced with new and unfamiliar conditions (O'Nions et al., 2020).

Avoid Confrontation

Conflicts between children with autism and their parents often occur. The trigger for conflict is usually the unruly behavior of children with autism. In addressing this issue, parents should be able to ascertain what routines the child likes. Following their preferred routine will reduce conflict and strengthen the social relationship between children and parents (Dawson-Squibb et al., 2020).

Use assistive devices

Parents can provide AAC (Augmentative and Alternative Communication) tools to help children communicate better (O'Nions et al., 2020).

Show positive feelings

Parents must be able to show positive feelings in educating children with autism. Happy and excited feelings are the key to creating social interaction between children and parents. Avoid negative feelings such as anger and annoyance towards children with autism. Education that is flavored with negative feelings will not create good social interaction, instead, the child will be confused by what his parents say (O'Nions et al., 2020).

B. Emotional and Financial Challenges for Families

Some studies shows that parents of children with autism are more stressed than parents of normal children. Unusual behavior in children with autism is what distinguishes them from normal children. Many parents can't cope with a child with autism. Feelings of guilt, fatigue, and anger often accompany parents in educating children with autism. So parents who have children with autism must get support from the people around them(Picardi et al., 2018) .

Parents who have children with autism also have to spend more funds on educating children with autism. The expensive cost of therapy is one of the challenges for parents in educating children with autism. In addition, parents who have children with autism must also be able to give more time to their children so that their working hours and income are reduced (Yaacob et al., 2021).

C. Sibling Perspectives on Living with Autism

Siblings of children with autism have unique perspectives. Positive feelings such as empathy and patience are usually shared by children whose siblings have autism. However, they can also have negative feelings such as shame, anger, and resentment towards their sibling. So children who have siblings with autism need to be educated by their parents. Parents should be able to explain about medical conditions and explain how to interact well with their siblings with autism (Schmeer et al., 2021).

D. Building Strong Family Support Systems

Strong family support is the key to success in educating children with autism. Families must be able to provide strong support for their children with autism. However, to be able to provide strong support, each family member must have an understanding of the medical condition suffered by one of their family members. A deep understanding of autism will lead to feelings of compassion so that families will be able to be patient in dealing with the unusual behavior of children with autism. After having a good understanding, families are required to always be there to assist because children with autism require more attention than other normal children. As a family, you must be able to love each other and support other family members (Bonfim et al., 2023).

References

Bonfim, T. de A., Giacon-Arruda, B. C. C., Galera, S. A. F., Teston, E. F., Nascimento, F. G. P. Do & Marcheti, M. A. (2023). Assistance to families of children with Autism Spectrum Disorders: Perceptions of the multiprofessional team. *Revista Latino-Americana de Enfermagem*, *31*, e3780. https://doi.org/10.1590/1518-8345.5694.3780

Bradshaw, J., Wolfe, K., Hock, R. & Scopano, L. (2022). Advances in Supporting Parents in Interventions for Autism Spectrum Disorder. *Pediatric Clinics of North America*, *69*(4), 645–656. https://doi.org/10.1016/j.pcl.2022.04.002

Dawson-Squibb, J.-J., Davids, E. L., Harrison, A. J., Molony, M. A. & de Vries, P. J. (2020). Parent Education and Training for autism spectrum disorders: Scoping the evidence. *Autism*, *24*(1), 7–25. https://doi.org/10.1177/1362361319841739

O'Nions, E., Ceulemans, E., Happé, F., Benson, P., Evers, K. & Noens, I. (2020). Parenting Strategies Used by Parents of Children with ASD: Differential Links with Child Problem Behaviour. *Journal of Autism and Developmental Disorders*, *50*(2), 386–401. https://doi.org/10.1007/s10803-019-04219-2

Picardi, A., Gigantesco, A., Tarolla, E., Stoppioni, V., Cerbo, R., Cremonte, M., Alessandri, G., Lega, I. & Nardocci, F. (2018). Parental Burden and its Correlates in Families of Children with Autism Spectrum Disorder: A Multicentre Study with Two Comparison Groups. *Clinical Practice & Epidemiology in*

Mental Health, 14(1), 143–176. https://doi.org/10.2174/1745017901814010143

Schmeer, A., Harris, V. W., Forthun, L., Valcante, G. & Visconti, B. (2021). Through the eyes of a child: Sibling perspectives on having a sibling diagnosed with autism. *Research in Developmental Disabilities, 119,* 104066. https://doi.org/10.1016/j.ridd.2021.104066

Yaacob, W. N. W., Yaacob, L. H., Muhamad, R. & Zulkifli, M. M. (2021). Behind the Scenes of Parents Nurturing a Child with Autism: A Qualitative Study in Malaysia. *International Journal of Environmental Research and Public Health, 18*(16), 8532. https://doi.org/10.3390/ijerph18168532.

CHAPTER 8: AUTISM IN ADULTHOOD

Akbar Triandra, Department of Medicine, Faculty of Medicine, Sriwijaya University

A. Transitioning to Independence: Challenges and Opportunities

For individuals with ASD, the transition to independence in adulthood is a complex and challenging phase. This includes aspects such as finding a job, living independently and establishing meaningful social relationships. Individuals with ASD often face significant barriers such as difficulties in social and executive functioning, communication limitations and access to adequate services. Their main challenge is to cope with new situations and process complex information that is an integral part of daily life independently. Adolescents with ASD reported a perceived level of personal independence of 22.9%, a significantly lower percentage compared to their peers. Lack of support from the surrounding community and the stigma associated with ASD often exacerbate this condition making it difficult for individuals with ASD to have equal opportunities in various aspects of life (Tadesse et al., 2024).

However, this transition also offers great opportunities for empowerment and improved quality of life. Structured supports, such as life skills training programs, employment assistance, and community-based interventions, can help individuals with ASD develop their full potential. Adaptive technologies and personalized facility approaches are also increasingly opening up opportunities to support the unique needs of each individual (Roux et al., 2024). With a holistic approach involving families, health professionals and communities, individuals with ASD can achieve meaningful independence and lead productive and inclusive lives in society.

B. Autism in the Workplace: Inclusion and Adaptation

Organizational interest in hiring individuals with ASD has increased. This interest is due in part to companies realizing the value of hiring employees with ASD. Research shows that employees with ASD typically pay close attention to detail, enjoy certain job tasks that other employees may find repetitive or socially isolating, and bring a different perspective to problems, which allows for innovative solutions to common problems. Research also shows that employees with ASD have high levels of trust, integrity and honesty. They are reliable, precise, efficient and consistent. Although individuals with ASD have skills, the unemployment and underemployment rates for these individuals, compared to the general population, remain very low. This difference suggests that it is critical to understand the employer's perspective and experience, so that hiring practices and outcomes can be improved for both organizations and employees with ASD (Griffiths et al., 2020).

For individuals with ASD, having a job is fulfilling and valuable. Overall, the level of family involvement, availability of vocational support services, and employers' willingness to integrate this group into their workforce are determinants for positive employment outcomes for individuals with ASD. Workplace inclusion is not just about accepting individuals with ASD, but also about understanding their specific needs (Zhou et al., 2024). In addition, it is important to educate coworkers about diversity and create an open and supportive environment. With the right adaptations, individuals with ASD can not only succeed in their jobs, but also feel valued and accepted in the team.

C. Relationships and Social Life for Adults with Autism

Recent studies have shown that individuals with ASD actively use various community platforms, both face-to-face and online, to practice and improve their social skills. In many cases, they choose environments that demand less verbal interaction so that they can be more comfortable in interacting with others (Morrison et al, 2020). The use of social media, for example, provides a space for individuals with ASD to expand their social networks, share experiences, and gain support from people who have more understanding of their condition. This is an important step to reduce social isolation and strengthen their engagement in social life (Chan, Doran & Galobardi, 2022).

In addition, involvement in the autism community allows individuals with ASD to find people who have similar experiences, creating stronger bonds due to mutual understanding of the challenges faced. In adulthood, many individuals with ASD find it easier to interact in groups with people who share similar experiences, as this reduces the stress that usually arises in social interactions with neurotypical people. An approach based on shared understanding and greater support for their specific needs can contribute significantly to the quality of their social relationships in the wider community.

D. Addressing the Needs of Older Adults on the Spectrum

Addressing the needs of older adults with ASD requires a deeper understanding of their experiences as they age. Many individuals with ASD face long-term mental health difficulties, such as depression, associated with cognitive decline in aging. Recent research suggests that individuals with ASD have greater health and mental health needs than the general population. Physical or mental health conditions are reported in 50-84% of ASD individuals, but little is known about the health and social support services available to older autistic adults, especially those who require ongoing support related to autistic traits, mental health difficulties, or daily living skills (Roestorf et al., 2019).

It is important to develop more specific and structured support for adults on the autism spectrum as they age. This support should include interventions that not only address basic autism-related needs, but also the impact of aging. In addition to appropriate medical care, such as physical and mental health management, creating a supportive and comfortable environment is crucial for older individuals on the autism spectrum (Heijnen-Kohl et al., 2022). Solutions to address these challenges include the provision of ongoing emotional and social support, as well as access to more holistic healthcare, which can help them manage the changes that come with aging.

References

Chan, D.V., Doran, J.D. and Galobardi, O.D. (2022). Beyond Friendship: The Spectrum of Social Participation of Autistic Adults. *Journal of Autism and Developmental Disorders*, 53(1). doi:https://doi.org/10.1007/s10803-022-05441-1.

Griffiths, A.J., Hanson, A.H., Giannantonio, C.M., Mathur, S.K., Hyde, K. and Linstead, E. (2020). Developing Employment Environments Where Individuals with ASD Thrive: Using Machine Learning to Explore Employer Policies and Practices. *Brain Sciences*, 10(9), p.632. doi:https://doi.org/10.3390/brainsci10090632.

Heijnen-Kohl, S.M.J., Hitzert, B., Schmidt, R., Geurts, H.M. and van Alphen, S.P.J. (2022). Features and Needs of Autistic Older Adults: A Delphi Study of Clinical Experiences. *Clinical Gerontologist*, pp.1–11. doi:https://doi.org/10.1080/07317115.2022.2060157.

Morrison, K.E., DeBrabander, K.M., Jones, D.R., Faso, D.J.,

Ackerman, R.A. and Sasson, N.J. (2019). Outcomes of real-world social interaction for autistic adults paired with autistic compared to typically developing partners. *Autism*, 24(5), pp.1067–1080. doi:https://doi.org/10.1177/1362361319892701.

Roestorf, A., Bowler, D.M., Deserno, M.K., Howlin, P., Klinger, L., McConachie, H., Parr, J.R., Powell, P., Van Heijst, B.F.C. and Geurts, H.M. (2019). 'Older Adults with ASD: The Consequences of Aging.' Insights from a series of special interest group meetings held at the International Society for Autism Research 2016–2017. *Research in Autism Spectrum Disorders*, 63, pp.3–12. doi:https://doi.org/10.1016/j.rasd.2018.08.007.

Roux, A.M., Chvasta, K., McLean, K.J., Carey, M., Liz, G.P., Tomczuk, L., Lopez, K., Evva Assing-Murray, Shattuck, P.T. and Shea, L.L. (2024). Challenges and Opportunities in Transitioning Autistic Individuals Into Adulthood. *PEDIATRICS*. doi:https://doi.org/10.1542/peds.2024-067195.

Tadesse, H., Desie, Y., Zeleke, W.A. and Habtamu, K. (2024). Challenges of transition to adolescence among children with autism spectrum disorder: an exploratory qualitative study of parents' and teachers' perspectives. *International Journal of Adolescence and Youth*, 29(1). doi:https://doi.org/10.1080/02673843.2024.2436058.

Zhou, K., Alam, B., Bani-Fatemi, A., Howe, A., Vijay Kumar Chattu and Behdin Nowrouzi-Kia (2024). Autism spectrum disorder in the workplace: a position paper to support an inclusive and neurodivergent approach to work participation and engagement. *Discover Psychology*, 4(1). doi:https://doi.org/10.1007/s44202-024-00150-5

CHAPTER 9: SOCIETAL AWARENESS AND INCLUSION

Yolanda Delia Putri, Department of Medicine, Faculty of Medicine, Sriwijaya University

A.   Understanding and Combating Stigma

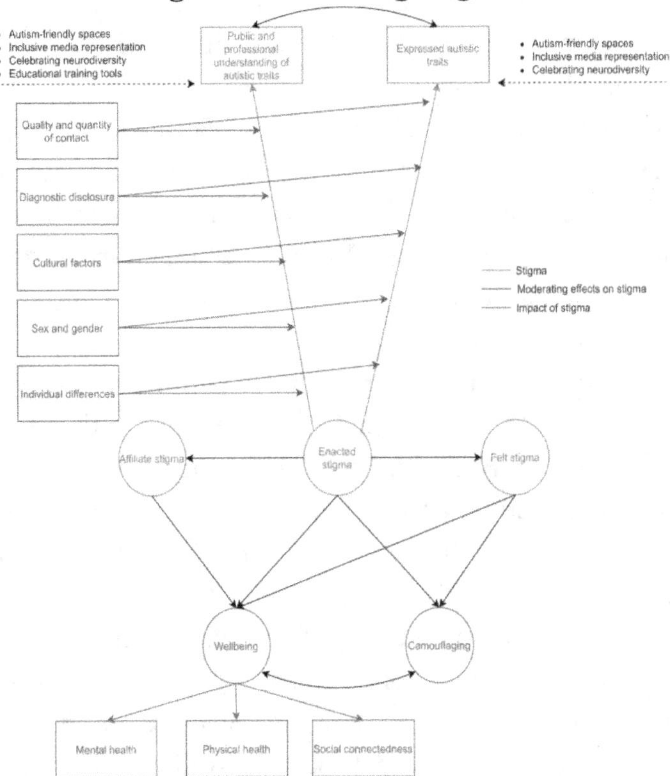

Figure 9.1. Theoretical model of causes and impact of autism stigma (Turnock et al., 2022)

Turnock et al. (2022) define stigma as a comprehensive term that encompasses three main aspects: knowledge problems (ignorance), attitude problems (prejudice), and behavioral problems (discrimination).

This stigma affects individuals across the autism spectrum, including those with severe autism. In this group, marginalization often occurs because communication challenges and intensive care needs can lead to different experiences of stigmatization (Clarke et al.,

2024).

In everyday life, individuals with Autism Spectrum Disorder (ASD) experience negative experiences that reflect this stigma. For example, neurotypical individuals, or individuals who are considered normal, tend to be reluctant to live in the same building as autistic individuals, make friends, and build intimate relationships with autistic individuals. In fact, in some cases, autistic individuals can also be inherited by neurotypical individuals (Turnock et al., 2022).

As detailed in Figure 9.1, key variables contributing to autism stigma include societal and professional understandings of autism traits and how they manifest. These understandings play a significant role in shaping and reinforcing stigma (Turnock et al., 2022).

Public and Professional Understanding of Autism Characteristics

Public and professional understanding of autism is often inadequate, which is compounded by negative attitudes and stigma towards autistic individuals. Examples include the belief that autism is always a symptom of other conditions, that all autistic children have poor eye contact, or that autistic individuals are unable to show affection or emotion.

Among healthcare professionals, misinformation and inadequate knowledge about autism become concerns. Although general practitioners in the UK demonstrate good knowledge of autism, many of them feel a lack of confidence in interacting with autistic individuals, which could be said to reflect the limited factual knowledge in equipping professionals to engage effectively with autistic individuals. Teachers and childcare providers often have poor knowledge and outdated beliefs, particularly about the causes of autism (etiology). This can have a direct impact on autistic students, who can sometimes feel stigmatized by their teachers. This stigma is often linked to judgments based on teachers' previous experiences with other autistic students.

This lack of understanding is largely due to a lack of formal training. Professionals with greater knowledge and experience tend to have more inclusive and less stigmatizing views of autistic individuals. Therefore, it is important to broaden the understanding of autism, including knowledge of how best to support and empower autistic individuals in various aspects of their lives (Turnock et al., 2022).

Expressing Autistic Traits

Social communication difficulties in autistic individuals are often reflected in physical behavior. Examples include unusual eye contact patterns, reduced facial expressions, limitations in sharing emotions, and limited use of gestures. In addition, they may exhibit restricted and repetitive behaviors, including specific motor behaviors or unusual responses to sensory stimuli. These sensory behaviors often become more pronounced in unfamiliar settings, where overwhelming sensory experiences can cause significant distress.

These visible autistic traits often influence first impressions. When assessed through video clips, neurotypical individuals tend to rate autistic individuals as less attractive, more submissive, and more awkward than their neurotypical peers. However, these biases did not emerge when only speech transcripts without visual stimuli were presented, suggesting that expressive differences are the primary drivers.

Some of these expressive differences, such as stereotyped or repetitive motor behaviors known as "stimming," are often negatively rated by neurotypical individuals. Autistic individuals feel that these behaviors make them feel strange or demeaned. Additionally, some autistic behavioral differences have also been reported as being something that may be seen as frightening by neurotypical individuals, adding challenges to their social interactions (Turnock et al., 2022).

Moderating Factors

The quality and quantity of interactions between autistic and neurotypical individuals have a significant impact on perceptions and attitudes of both groups. Knowing and spending time with autistic individuals has been shown to correlate with more positive attitudes toward autistic children and adults. For neurotypical individuals, high-quality interactions can reduce anxiety and increase comfort, which in turn reinforces a better understanding and attitude toward autism.

Conversely, high-quality interactions also provide benefits for autistic individuals. They help them feel more comfortable, creating an environment that allows for a more accurate understanding of their condition. However, a lack of understanding and negative attitudes from neurotypical individuals can trigger less pleasant social interactions, such as being treated unkindly. These reactions can make autistic individuals feel wary, limiting opportunities for meaningful social relationships and reinforcing stigma.

Additionally, because autism is not associated with distinctive physical characteristics, autistic individuals' unique behaviors are often perceived as social deviations rather than underlying differences or challenges. This combination of "normal" appearance and unconventional behaviors can reinforce stigma in society.

Overall, the quality of interactions had a more significant impact than the quantity of interactions. Therefore, focusing on improving the quality of contact between autistic and neurotypical individuals is key to reducing stigma and building better relationships. Cultural factors have a significant influence on autism stigma, including the perception, understanding, and expression of autism traits:

1. Cultural Stigma

   The level of stigma varies across cultures. Individualistic cultures, such as the United States, tend to have lower stigma than collectivist cultures such as Lebanon, Japan, and China. In Japan, despite a good understanding of autism, cultural norms that emphasize group cohesion over individual needs contribute to high levels of stigma toward autism.

2. The Influence of Labels and Cultural Beliefs

   - In South Korea, labels such as "border children" are used to avoid the stigma of an autism diagnosis.

- In China, cultural pressures to be successful in boys lead some parents to hide an autism diagnosis.
- In Vietnam and certain African countries, autism is often associated with illness, bad karma, or supernatural phenomena, which increases stigma and fuels harmful practices in "healing."

3. Minority Communities
   - In the United Kingdom, Somali families often hide their autistic children because they face high stigma.
   - In the United States, Black communities face stigma caused by shame, denial, and racism in the diagnosis process.
   - In Australia, Aboriginal communities report stigma stemming from cultural shame and discrimination from non-Aboriginal groups.

4. Cultural Influences on Autism Expression
   The expression of autism traits varies across cultures and is often influenced by local social norms:
   - Autistic girls report pressure to conform to gender stereotypes, such as expected social skills, making them more vulnerable to stigma. They also feel punished more often in social interactions than autistic boys and neurotypical individuals.
   - Autistic girls are more likely to feel like victims in peer groups than autistic boys or neurotypical children.

5. Stigma toward Parents of Autistic Children
   Mothers of autistic children are more likely to experience stigma than fathers, including avoidance, hostile stares, and negative comments from the community. This is related to gender stereotypes that place higher expectations on the mother's parenting role (Turnock et al., 2022).

Reducing Autism Stigma

A variety of approaches have been developed to reduce stigma toward people with autism and their families, although research on their effectiveness is limited. Some approaches that may have positive impacts include (Turnock et al., 2022):

1. *Autism-Friendly Spaces*

   Autism-friendly spaces are designed to increase social and physical comfort for people with autism. Examples include quiet spaces, appropriate lighting, and clear settings for social interactions. These spaces allow people with autism to integrate more easily into the community and minimize pressure to conform, allowing them to express themselves authentically. Although not empirically tested, these spaces are thought to improve understanding and attitudes toward autism.

2. Educational and Psychosocial Training Tools

   - Formal Training: PowerPoint-based online training has increased knowledge and reduced stigma, although its long-term impact is unknown. Autism acceptance training videos have also shown positive effects on social relationships and self-reported stigma, but not implicit bias.

   - Educational Programs for Children: Programs such as Understanding Our Peers with Pablo help improve attitudes towards unfamiliar autistic children but have limited impact on positive behavioral intentions towards familiar autistic peers.

   - Simulated Autism Experiences: Technologies such as Auti-Sim create simulated sensory overload, which increases empathy and helping intentions, although they have little effect on explicit attitudes towards autism. Videos of everyday experiences of people with autism have also shown positive impacts on empathy.

   - Comprehensive Approaches: School programs such as Learning with Autism in Wales involve the whole organization and can lead to wider cultural change towards autism inclusion.

3. Direct Input from People with Autism

Including input from people with autism in the development of training tools increases their effectiveness in changing knowledge, reducing stigma, and improving attitudes towards inclusion.

B.   The Role of Media in Shaping Autism Awareness

Knowing someone with autism is often associated with more positive attitudes and reduced stigma. Knowledge about autism can be improved through broader and more accurate representation in the media. Studies have shown that negative reporting of autism correlates with negative attitudes, while positive representation can reduce stigma. Unfortunately, media portrayals are often negative or inaccurate, despite calls for more balanced representation that reflects the diversity of the autism spectrum (Turnock et al., 2022).

Benefits of Positive Representation

Positive portrayals can support autistic individuals and their families by increasing public understanding. The presence of autistic role models in the media and an emphasis on diverse experiences can help reduce the need to "camouflage" or hide their autistic traits, which can have positive impacts on their well-being (Turnock et al., 2022).

Media's Influence on Public Perception

The media is one of the primary sources of information about mental health and neurodivergence, such as autism. In addition to reflecting public opinion, the media also has the power to shape it. Negative portrayals can reinforce stigma and stereotypes, while more supportive narratives can increase recognition and understanding of autism, improving overall societal attitudes (Bakombo et al., 2023).

The Role of Social Media

Social media, such as Facebook, Twitter, TikTok, YouTube,

and Reddit, play a significant role in influencing public perceptions of autism. These platforms allow communities to share experiences, interact, and collaborate, creating diverse community-based input. The content shared, whether factual or opinionated, can significantly shape public views. For example, research exploring the representation of autistic individuals' experiences on YouTube suggests that public engagement through comments can influence audiences' views of autism.

Thus, media has great potential to educate and reduce stigma if managed appropriately. An emphasis on more balanced and empathetic portrayals of autism could have a broader positive impact on society (Bakombo et al., 2023).

C. Advocacy and Autism Rights Movements
Neurodiversity Movement

The neurodiversity movement focuses on changing society's view of autism from a deficit to a difference that enriches human diversity. This principle is based on the minority model of disability, which emphasizes that social barriers, not individual conditions, create disability. The movement rejects the medical model that views autism as a deficit, instead viewing it as a difference that makes a positive contribution. A neurodiversity-supportive view has been linked to reduced stigma around autism, increased self-esteem, and decreased anxiety and depression in autistic individuals. The use of identity-first language, such as "autistic individuals" rather than "individuals with autism," is also considered less stigmatizing (Turnock et al., 2022).

Neurodiversity advocates for a paradigm shift in research and professional practice, including the use of terms such as "autism spectrum condition" to replace "autism spectrum disorder." The movement supports the acceptance of autistic behaviors, such as stimming, and encourages activities that showcase the accomplishments of autistic people, especially when designed by the autistic community itself. By promoting this acceptance, the neurodiversity movement creates an inclusive culture that allows autistic individuals to express themselves authentically without having to disguise their behavior. Potential impacts include increased public understanding, reduced stigma, and improved mental health for autistic individuals (Turnock et al., 2022).

D. Creating an Inclusive Society for All

The intervention framework for autism is closely aligned with the vision of creating an inclusive society for all. Inclusion means building an environment where every individual, regardless of ability or challenges, can participate fully in social, educational, and community life. Intervention strategies that target the child, family, school, and community create a foundation for this vision (Bondy & Weiss, 2013).

Inclusive Society Through Tailored Support

An inclusive society recognizes the unique needs of individuals with autism and supports their development through targeted interventions. By addressing core deficits in autism, such as communication and social interaction, interventions empower children to engage meaningfully with peers. This approach ensures that they are not only accepted but also prepared to thrive in their social environment (Bondy & Weiss, 2013).

The Role of Family, School, and Community

- Families play a critical role in creating inclusive spaces by supporting the child's development and the new skills they acquire. Strong family involvement ensures continuity of learning and strengthens relationships that create a sense of belonging.
- Schools serve as miniature communities, where inclusive practices, such as peer-based models and supportive environments, enable children with autism to participate as equals. In these environments, neurotypical peers also learn

about empathy and diversity, fostering acceptance on a broader scale.

- Communities serve as the final stage of inclusion, where individuals with autism can apply their skills to meaningfully contribute to the development of society. Through community-based opportunities, such as service programs or social initiatives, communities reinforce the value of inclusion while reducing stigma (Bondy & Weiss, 2013).

Inclusion as a Multilevel Effort

Inclusion requires addressing systemic barriers. For children with autism, this means providing interventions tailored to their developmental trajectories and specific social contexts. By integrating efforts at the individual, family, educational, and community levels, communities move toward a holistic model of inclusion (Bondy & Weiss, 2013).

References

Bakombo, S., Ewalefo, P., & Konkle, A. T. M. (2023). The Influence of Social Media on the Perception of Autism Spectrum Disorders: Content Analysis of Public Discourse on YouTube Videos. *International Journal of Environmental Research and Public Health,* *20*(4), 3246. https://doi.org/10.3390/ijerph20043246

Bondy, A., & Weiss, M. J. (2013). *Teaching social skills to people with autism : best practices in individualizing interventions* (Vol. 5). Woodbine House.

Clarke, E. B., McCauley, J. B., Lutz, A., Gotelli, M., Sheinkopf, S. J., & Lord, C. (2024). Understanding profound autism: implications for stigma and supports. *Frontiers in Psychiatry,* *15*. https://doi.org/10.3389/fpsyt.2024.1287096

Turnock, A., Langley, K., & Jones, C. R. G. (2022). Understanding Stigma in Autism: A Narrative Review and Theoretical Model. *Autism in Adulthood,* *4*(1), 76–91.

https://doi.org/10.1089/aut.2021.0005

CHAPTER 10: THE FUTURE OF AUTISM RESEARCH

Adinda Nezma Meidina, Department of Medicine, Faculty of Medicine, Sriwijaya University

A. Advances in Genetics and Neuroscience Research

Genetic Discoveries Related to Autism

Recent studies have shown the important role of genetic variation in the etiology of autism. Many researchers have proposed new insights into the genetic basis of ASD and further studies have proven the role of genes in the basic pathophysiology of ASD. Genetic variation is known to be involved in mitochondrial dysfunction, abnormal neurodevelopment, and dysfunction of neurodevelopmental stability. Table 10.1. describes the role of genes involved in the pathophysiology of ASD (Fang et al., 2023).

Table 10.1. The role of genes involved in the pathophysiology of ASD (Fang et al., 2023)

Gen	Peran Gen
CNTNAP2	Encodes a synaptic protein that is an important member of the neurexin superfamily.
	Plays a major role in neural development, and is essential for the assembly of neural circuits.
	*CNTNAP2 mutations cause functional impairment of synaptic neurotransmission, which may be associated with abnormal behavior in ASD.
	*CNTNAP2 rs2710102 has been shown to correlate with ASD risk
MTHFR	A key enzyme in the folate metabolism pathway, and plays a critical role in the conversion of cysteine to methionine and DNA synthesis.
	*Patients with ASD often have high plasma homocysteine levels and reduced methylation capacity.

	*MTHFR C677T and A1298C are associated with decreased enzyme activity.
OXTR	Encodes the oxytocin receptor, plays a key role in regulating social behavior. *Controversial results regarding the association of OXTR rs2254298 polymorphism and ASD risk.
VDR	Vitamin D plays a biological role by acting on the vitamin D receptor. Vitamin D is an essential nutrient in the human body and has potential effects on brain homeostasis and development, such as neuronal differentiation and neuronal migration *VDRrs731236 (Taq-I) and rs1544410 (Bsm-I) correlate with ASD risk

Brain Studies and Neurological Differences

Research shows that structural and volume abnormalities of the brain are the most consistent features of ASD. Table 10.2. explains structural brain abnormalities in children with ASD based on MRI images (Dougherty et al., 2015).

Table 10. 2. Structural brain abnormalities in children with ASD (Dougerty et al., 2015)

Brain region	ASD	
	Endophenotype	**Implicated phenotypes**
Total brain volume	Increased volume shortly after birth with arrest in growth in adolescence	Insufficient research
Cortical thickness	Unclear	Insufficient research
Temporal lobe	increased volume in childhood, possible decreases into adulthood	Insufficient research
Prefrontal cortex	Increased volume, possible reductions in OFC	Inattention, impulsivity, social deficits

Amygdala	Increased volume	Social deficits, emotional processing deficits
Corpus callosum	Reduced volume into adulthood	Insufficient research
Basal ganglia	Increased volume, caudate most often implicated	Repetitive and stereotyped behaviors
Cerebellum	Decreased volume mostly in children	Attention, impaired motor coordination

Genetic Technologies and Potential Therapies

In recent years, gene therapy has emerged as a promising approach for treating various diseases, including ASD. CRISPR-Cas9 is a gene therapy tool capable of genetic silencing through non-homologous end joining or correcting genetic mutations via homologous recombination. This advancement offers new hope for the treatment of genetically linked conditions, including ASD. Figure 10.1 illustrates the structure and function of the clustered regularly interspaced short palindromic repeats-associated protein 9 (CRISPR-Cas9) technique in autism spectrum disorders. In this scheme, CRISPR-Cas9 recognizes target sequences using adjacent protospacer adjacent motifs (PAM) and induces cuts at specific points (Sandhu, 2023).

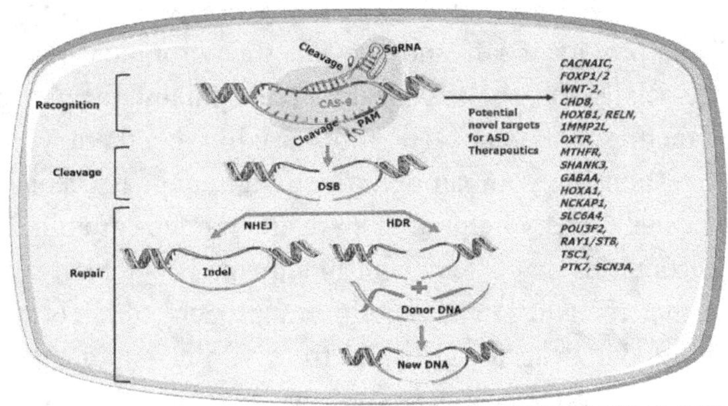

DOI: 10.12998/wjcc.v11.i14.3114 Copyright ©The Author(s) 2023.

Figure 10. 1. The structure and functioning of CRISPR-Cas9 in ASD (Sandhu, 2023)

B. The Role of Technology in Autism Support

Virtual Reality

Virtual reality (VR) technology is increasingly being used in the treatment of Autism Spectrum Disorder (ASD). By utilizing a controlled virtual environment, VR provides an opportunity for individuals with ASD to practice social, communication, and sensory management skills. For example, VR can simulate everyday life situations, so that individuals with autism can practice interactions, such as recognizing facial expressions, speaking, or reading social cues, in a safe, anxiety-free environment. The technology also allows for adjustments to the level of sensory stimulation to reduce anxiety or confusion. In addition, VR therapy allows for repeated practice, which is very helpful in reinforcing skills that have been learned. With a more engaging and personalized approach, VR can support individuals with ASD in developing the skills needed to live more independently and confidently (Maddalon, 2024).

Robot-Assisted Therapy (RAAT)

Robot-Assisted Therapy (RAAT) has shown great potential in supporting the treatment of children with autism, by utilizing robotic technology to improve social interaction, communication, and emotional skills. Based on a systematic review of existing research, RAAT can provide a safe and controlled environment for children to practice social skills, such as speaking, recognizing facial expressions, and interacting with peers. The robot used in this therapy is designed to be a responsive companion, which can adapt its behavior to the child's needs, thereby helping them overcome the communication and social difficulties that often occur in autism. This therapy also allows for a more personalized and repetitive approach, which is essential for reinforcing skill learning. Results from various studies have shown that RAAT can effectively improve the social and emotional skills of children with autism, making it a promising alternative in autism treatment (Alabdulkareem et al., 2022).

References

Alabdulkareem, A., Alhakbani, N., & Al-Nafjan, A. (2022). A Systematic Review of Research on Robot-Assisted Therapy for Children with Autism. *Sensors*, *22*(3), 944. https://doi.org/10.3390/s22030944

Dougherty, C. C., Evans, D. W., Myers, S. M., Moore, G. J., & Michael, A. M. (2015). A Comparison of Structural Brain Imaging Findings in Autism Spectrum Disorder and Attention-Deficit Hyperactivity Disorder. *Neuropsychology Review*, 26(1), 25–43. https://doi.org/10.1007/s11065-015-9300-2

Fang, Y., Cui, Y., Yin, Z., Hou, M., Guo, P., Wang, H., Liu, N., Cai, C., & Wang, M. (2023). Comprehensive systematic review and meta-analysis of the association between common genetic variants and autism spectrum disorder. *Gene, 887*, 147723–147723. https://doi.org/10.1016/j.gene.2023.147723.

Maddalon, L., Minissi, M. E., Parsons, T., Hervas, A., & Alcaniz, M. (2024). Exploring Adaptive Virtual Reality Systems Used in Interventions for Children With Autism Spectrum Disorder: Systematic Review. *Journal of Medical Internet Research*, 26, e57093. https://doi.org/10.2196/57093

Sandhu, A., Kumar, A., Rawat, K., Gautam, V., Sharma, A., & Saha, L. (2023). Modernising autism spectrum disorder model engineering and treatment via CRISPR-Cas9: A gene reprogramming approach. *World Journal of Clinical Cases*, 11(14), 3114–3127. https://doi.org/10.12998/wjcc.v11.i14.3114

ABOUT THE AUTHOR

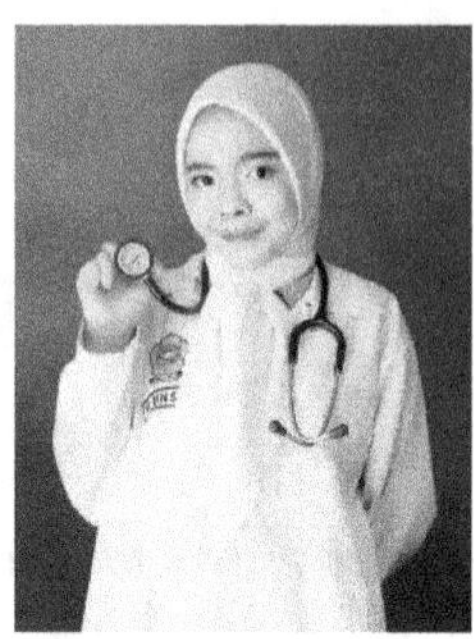

Adinda Nezma Meidina, the main author of this book, was born in Jambi on May 17, 2004. She is an active figure in research and writing as a medical student at the Faculty of Medicine, Sriwijaya University. She has won three gold medals in international innovation competitions and has achieved several accolades at the national level in scientific writing. Currently, she serves as a member of the Core Management Board of the BAPIN-ISMKI organization, a scientific institution that oversees all medical faculty scientific institutions across Indonesia. She has three journal publications as the lead author and two books indexed ISBN under her main author. Additionally, she is involved in humanitarian activities, including coordinating a free health check-up event in South Sumatra, which attracted more than 600 participants. Due to her achievements, she was honored with the Outstanding Youth of South Sumatra Province Award in 2024.

Nafilah Ramadhanti, a medical student at Universitas Sriwijaya, is highly dedicated to academic pursuits. She actively participates in writing competitions and scientific research, focusing on solutions to health challenges in Indonesia. In addition to her academic contributions, Nafilah is also involved in various organizations, such as the Forum Kajian Ilmiah dan Akademik FK Unsri, AMSA-Unsri, and BEM KM FK Unsri, expanding her contributions in the fields of medicine and health.

Raisa Qonita, is a medical student from Faculty of Medicine, Universitas Sriwijaya who has excelled in the field of scientific achievement, as demonstrated by her Gold Medal wins in prestigious international competitions such as the International Young Moslem Inventors Awards (IYMIA), the International Invention Competition for Young Moslem Scientists (IICYMS), and the Global Youth Invention Competition (GYIC). She also earned Third Place in the Scientific Poster Competition at SPECTRUM 2023 at the faculty level. In addition to her academic achievements, Raisa is actively involved in community service through various social outreach programs, reflecting her dedication and compassion. Her organizational skills are evident in her key roles as General Treasurer of FKIA FK UNSRI for 2023/2024 and Deputy Head of the Information and Communication Department of BEM KM FK UNSRI. Through these positions, Raisa has showcased her expertise in financial management and communication, contributing significantly to the success of her organizations.

M. Aditya Nugraha, is a student of FK UNSRI who is active in academics and research. He has published a journal entitled "The Role of Implementing the HPV Vaccination Program with Optimization of Cervical Cancer Screening and Treatment as an Ambitious Strategy to Reduce the Prevalence of Cervical Cancer in Developing Countries: A Literature Review" with his team. In addition, he and his team won a gold medal in the IICYMS competition through a journal entitled "trusT-B: Integrative, Educative, and Assistive e-Health Application as A Preventive Strategy on The Rise of Suspect and Patient of TBC to Achieve SDG's 30". Aditya was also a finalist in the Lupus Olympiad organized by the Indonesian Rheumatology Association in 2024 and a finalist in the RMO Neuropsychiatry competition in the same year, showing his dedication to the fields of medicine and health innovation.

Nabila Az-zahra Hasibuan, a student who is active in student activities, by joining the Student Executive Board (BEM) FK Unsri and the Sriwijaya Medical Assistance Team (TBM), shows her commitment to self-development and community service. In addition, she has also been involved in a publication entitled "The Potential of Zinc Oxide Metal Nanoparticle Technology (NP-ZnO) on Anti-TB Drugs as the Latest Modality for the Treatment of Multidrug-Resistant Tuberculosis (MDR-TB)", which shows her interest in academics and research in the health sector.

Dyah Fatha Istiqomah, a medical student at the Faculty of Medicine, University of Sriwijaya, who is not only active in academics but also plays a role in various organizations and volunteer activities. She is a member of the Student Executive Board of the Faculty of Medicine, University of Sriwijaya, as the treasurer of the Advocacy and Student Welfare Department, a department that focuses on internal and external student problems, where she excels in managing and administering finances, especially in that department. This also shows her contribution and concern for the sustainability of the lectures of the Faculty of Medicine, University of Sriwijaya students, and shows her dedication to improving lectures in the future. Her membership in the Sriwijaya Medical Assistance Team organization shows her broader devotion to the community regarding health issues. Writing, reading, and drawing are not only hobbies for Dyah but also part of her stages to develop and express her ideas.

Putri Salsabillah is an active student at the Faculty of Medicine, Sriwijaya University (FK Unsri). Putri shows high dedication to the world of education and organizations. In addition to focusing on medical studies, Putri is also actively involved in various organizations on campus. Putri joined the Student Executive Board (BEM) FK Unsri, BPPM Asy-Syifa FK Unsri and IKMB Unsri, where she contributed to various programs aimed at improving the quality of student life and facilitating self-development activities. The balance between lectures and organizational activities is proof that Putri has a high spirit in pursuing achievements and expanding her horizons.

Muhammad Valdis Muyassar, a student of FK UNSRI who has the ambition to change the education system in Indonesia. His experience in writing scientific papers, participating in olympiads, and seeking scholarships since high school reflects his dedication in achieving higher education. The density of medical studies did not prevent him from being active in organizations. By participating in the Sriwijaya Medical Assistance Team organization, FK UNSRI also shows his commitment to serving the community. In addition, his interest in writing books reflects his intention to share knowledge through the medium of writing.

Akbar Triandra, is a student who is actively involved in various student activities, both academic and non-academic. He demonstrates a strong dedication to self-development by participating in scientific competitions and producing several written works. Additionally, Akbar is engaged in community development activities, where he contributes by implementing programs that have a positive impact on the local environment, using his knowledge to create relevant and practical solutions.

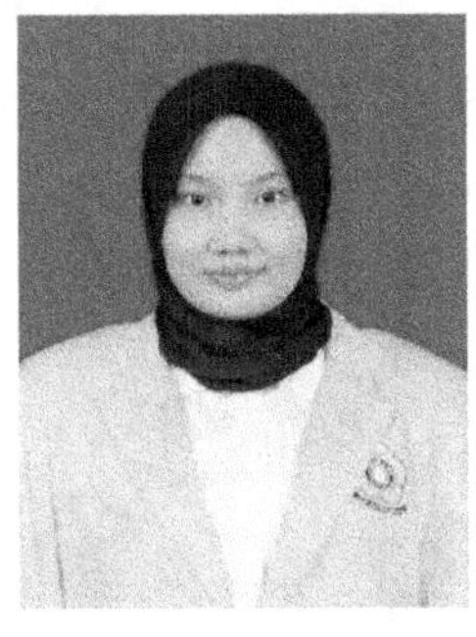

Yolanda Delia Putri, is a medical student at the Faculty of Medicine, Sriwijaya University who is active in academic and organizational activities within the faculty. Since 2023, she has been a member of the Sriwijaya Medical Assistance Team (TBMS) and has been actively involved in various work programs that focus on community service, such as TBMS Peduli Akbar and Community Development 2024. Through organizational education and training, she has acquired various medical skills such as emergency management, resuscitation, intubation, circumcision, among others. In addition, together with her team, she won a gold medal in an international competition with the theme of innovation in the field of medicine, which aims to improve the quality of public health.